Jewish Cracow

Eugeniusz Duda

JEWISH CRACOW

A Guide to the Historical Buildings and Places of Remembrance

Photography
Jacek Balcewicz

vis-à-vis
etiuda
KRAKÓW 2010

Copyright © by Eugeniusz Duda, Cracow
Copyright © for this edition by vis-à-vis/Etiuda, Cracow 2010
Second edition, revised and updated

Photography:
Jacek Balcewicz

Cover design:
Dariusz Zieliński

Graphic design:
Joanna Dzierzbicka

Text prepared for publication by:
Przemysław Dzierzbicki

Maps of Kazimierz by:
Firma Rysunkowa Szelerewicz

New edition updated and translated:
Mark Aldridge

Original translation:
Mark Aldridge and Kaja Kozłowska

The publishers wish to thank the City of Kraków Museum of History and the Kraków
Ethnographic Museum for access to archive photographs.

ISBN: 978-83-61516-41-5

Wydawnictwo vis-à-vis/Etiuda
30-549 Kraków, ul. Traugutta 16b/9
tel/fax: 012 4235274, tel. 600442702
e-mail: biuro@etiuda.net
www.etiuda.net

Printed by Drukarnia Colonel, Kraków

CONTENTS

INTRODUCTION

An exceptionally large number of historical buildings and monuments associated with Jewish history and culture survive in Kraków. The majority are in Kazimierz, where the unique framework of the old Jewish town, which flourished from the end of the fourteenth century to the middle of the nineteenth, has survived. The most important historical buildings and sites are the Old, Remu (New), High, Popper, Isaac and Kupa synagogues and the old cemetery around the Remu synagogue. But it is not only in Kazimierz that important Jewish historical buildings have survived in Kraków. A good deal less venerable than Kazimierz's synagogues they are the structural remains of the multifaceted growth and development of Jewish society in the nineteenth and twentieth centuries. Good examples are the Tempel or Progressive, synagogue on Ul. Miodowa and, on Ul. Skawińska, the headquarters of the Jewish town council and the building that used to house the Jewish hospital. But throughout the city there are many more educational, cultural, charitable and sporting historical buildings and sites built by Kraków's Jews. Few traces of its Jewish past have survived in Kazimierz's neighbouring Stradom district, which was settled only in the second half of the nineteenth century and in the twentieth, or in the city centre. Though it is true that Jews were already present in Kraków's old town in the thirteenth century, by the end of the fifteenth they had been expelled. They were to return only in the second half of the nineteenth century after securing citizenship rights. Remembering that it was precisely Kraków's main market square (Rynek Główny) that was the first site of institutionalised Jewish life in the city we begin our journey of exploration there. Leaving Rynek Główny via Ul. Grodzka and, moving on through Stradom to Kazimierz and the old Jewish town, we are tracing the steps taken at the end of the fifteenth century by expelled Kraków Jews and those of many of their descendants returning in the opposite direction in the nineteenth century as full citizens.

The first section has been divided into two routes:

1. Rynek Główny – Ulica Bocheńska
2. Ulica Józefa – Ulica Przemyska

In the Podgórze district, on the right bank of the Wisła, lie sites, relics and monuments of the extermination of the Kraków Jews in the Second World War. We visit this area, the ghetto and the Płaszów concentration camp following a third route:

3. Plac Bohaterów Getta – Płaszów

All three routes can be completed in a day. But for those who have only a few hours, we suggest visiting the most important monuments and historical buildings that are the subject of Route 2. These may be found on the pages marked in green.

Important: do not visit these places on the Sabbath (from sundown on Fridays to sundown on Saturdays) or on Jewish holidays as the cemeteries and synagogues are closed at these times. Men should be aware that to enter a synagogue or cemetery they must be wearing headgear.

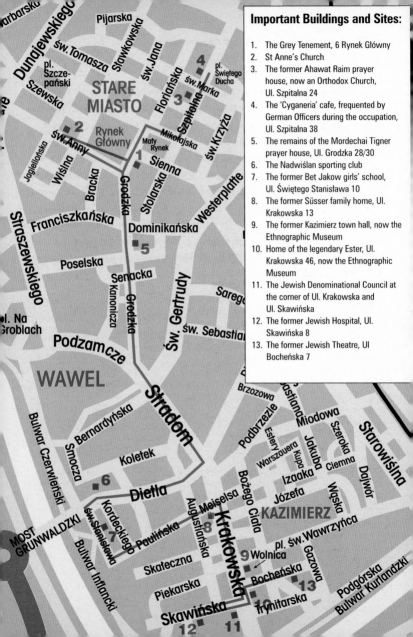

Important Buildings and Sites:

1. The Grey Tenement, 6 Rynek Główny
2. St Anne's Church
3. The former Ahawat Raim prayer house, now an Orthodox Church, Ul. Szpitalna 24
4. The 'Cyganeria' cafe, frequented by German Officers during the occupation, Ul. Szpitalna 38
5. The remains of the Mordechai Tigner prayer house, Ul. Grodzka 28/30
6. The Nadwiślan sporting club
7. The former Bet Jakow girls' school, Ul. Świętego Stanisława 10
8. The former Süsser family home, Ul. Krakowska 13
9. The former Kazimierz town hall, now the Ethnographic Museum
10. Home of the legendary Ester, Ul. Krakowska 46, now the Ethnographic Museum
11. The Jewish Denominational Council at the corner of Ul. Krakowska and Ul. Skawińska
12. The former Jewish Hospital, Ul. Skawińska 8
13. The former Jewish Theatre, Ul Bocheńska 7

ROUTE 1:

RYNEK GŁÓWNY – ULICA BOCHEŃSKA

ynek Główny, which measures 200×200 m, is the largest and most beautiful in Kraków and, alongside St Mark's square in Venice, is considered the very best of its kind in the world. What is more, it has been pulsating with life as the city's centre for more than seven centuries. It was laid out in 1257 when Prince Bolesław V the Chaste granted the city new settlement privileges based on Magdeburg city law. Into the geometric, chessboard pattern of Rynek Główny – off which the majority of streets lead at right angles – jut Romanesque buildings, built before Bolesław's privileges were granted, such as the Mariacki church, which was reconstructed in its present form in the years 1392–97. The church features a wooden, late-gothic altar, sculpted in the years 1477–89 by the Nuremberg master, Wit Stwosz. On the hour, every hour, from the church's high tower, resounds the *hejnał,* or bugle-call, known to all Poles as it is broadcast on national radio everyday at noon.

Rynek Główny was once a densely built-up area with, among other buildings, a gothic town hall and tower, a renaissance granary, the great scales, a foundry, market stalls and the trading place of the cloth hall which still stands today. Now in this monumental edifice, whose oldest section is Roman and which was rebuilt in the sixteenth century and then restored and put in order in the nineteenth, buying and selling is limited to the ground floor, as the first floor is occupied by the National Museum's Gallery of Polish painting. Among the works of eminent artists on display are those of Maurycy Gottlieb (1856–79) one of the most celebrated Polish painters of Jewish origin. Returning to buildings, there are two more from earlier periods in Rynek Główny to mention: the small, tenth century church of St Wojciech and the 'orphaned' town hall tower, all that remains of the fourteenth century structure that was demolished in the nineteenth century. It was outside St Wojciech's that the papal emissary, Jan Kapistrano, made a fiery speech against the Jews during his stay in 1453.

A far more recent structure, but one nevertheless already firmly rooted in the landscape of Rynek Główny, is the statue of the great poet Adam Mickiewicz, who was known for his pro-Jewish disposition. The monument was the work of Teodor Rygier. Completed in 1898, it was destroyed by the Germans in 1940 and then rebuilt in 1955.

The people of Kraków have witnessed a variety of state occasions in Rynek Główny. In 1525 Albrecht von Hohenzollern, the Prince of Prussia, paid homage to King Zygmunt I. The occasion also saw the King bestowing favours on more than a few of his subjects. One of the beneficiaries was the Jew, Michał Ezofowicz, who was the chief collector of taxes levied on Jews in Lithuania. He was ennobled and given the Leliwa coat of arms. Ezofowicz remained loyal to his faith and was the only titled, unchristened Jew in the history of the First Republic. The site of Hohenzollern's oath – where Ul. Bracka meets Rynek Główny – is marked by a commemorative plaque saying, 'The Prussian Homage 1525'.

A powerful demonstration of patriotism was Tadeusz Kościuszko's oath to the Polish nation of 24 March 1794 that began the rising against Russia. Kościuszko also appealed to the Jews to take part declaring that they would receive equal citizenship rights. The site of Kościuszko's oath, between the town hall tower and Ul. Szewska, is marked by a commemorative plaque.

But Rynek Główny, for all its buildings and the homes of the townspeople surrounding it, was always primarily a place of ceaseless trade and its attendant activities. Jewish shopkeepers and merchants, who have always played an important role in Kraków business,

The 'grey' tenement at 6 Rynek Główny

of a polonised Jewish family called the Feintuchs. In 1894 they took the name of the tenement, Szarski. Their shop, which sold imported goods, remained on this site until 1955 when it was closed down by the then government because of its 'reluctance' to countenance private entrepreneurial activity.

During different periods of the seventeenth and eighteenth centuries Jews kept shops in the Hipolite tenements at number three Plac Mariacki, in the Hetman tenements at number seventeen Rynek Główny and at Pod Baranami on the corner of the Rynek Główny and Ul. św. Anny. They also kept shops in buildings that are no longer standing such as the town hall and the weigh station.

The Jews were among the pioneers of book selling in Poland. But in Kraków in 1806 it was made illegal for them to sell door-to-door. Instead, they were allowed to sell second hand books on Rynek Główny around St Wojciech's church, in the passage of the Hetman tenement and in the back yard of the 'grey' tenement. After 1836 this trade was moved to Plac św. Ducha.

were fully engaged in this. Traditionally, they occupied Rynek Główny between Mickiewicz's statue and St Wojciech's church. Otherwise, they rented shops and storehouses in many of the buildings on the square and in the adjacent streets. So, for example, at number six, Jewish shops and warehouses had been present for a very long time – both at the front and in the yards of the building. Known as the 'grey' tenement number six was, in fact, once the property of magnate families, among them the Zebrzydowskis, the Zborowskis and the Czartoryskis, and is also remembered as the main headquarters of Kościuszko's 1794 rising and as the seat of the National Government in 1846. From the middle of the nineteenth century the house passed into the hands

Ul. Szpitalna: former centre of Jewish antiquarian bookshops

Before leaving Rynek Główny it is essential to visit two of the streets leading off it: św. Anny and Ul. Szpitalna. Moving down św. Anny, which leads from Rynek Główny to the university quarter, we reach the crossroads with Ul. Jagiellońska – the site of the Jagiellonian University's oldest college, Collegium Maius, which now houses the University Museum. The college had its beginnings in a stone house on the corner of Jegiellońska and Anny, which was bought expressly to found a college on the instructions of King Władysław Jagiełło. At that time, the area in and around św.

Anny, from Rynek Główny to the city walls, was occupied by Jews. They had been there since at least the second half of the thirteenth century and their property was, rather than being segregated off in one particular block, fully mixed in with that owned by Christians. As the University expanded, though, it gradually bought up the Jewish properties. The last of these, which included a synagogue and other buildings used in common by the Jews, was purchased in 1469. The Jews then moved to the area around św. Tomasza and Plac Szczepański on the north-west side of Rynek Główny.

13

The Former Ahawat Raim prayer house, now an Orthodox Church, Ul. Szpitalna 24

Rising above the right-hand side of św Anny is the eponymous St Anne's church, which was built to its present form in the years 1689-1705 by Tylman van Gameren on land that had been the site of two earlier churches.

This is a place with profound associations for the Kraków Jews as the flashpoint for the 1407 pogrom. This event is described in detail in Canon Jan Długosz's Chronicles of Kraków. Św. Anny leads out to the Planty, the green space surrounding the old town around the old fortifications. There, in the mediaeval city wall, was the Jewish Gate through which the Jews passed into the cemetery on the site of what is today Ul. Czysta. Of this cemetery, and of the mediaeval synagogues of Kraków, no traces remain.

From św. Anny we return to Rynek Główny, cut a diagonal path across it in the direction of the Mariacki Church and the Mały Rynek (the small market square), and enter Ul. Szpitalna at the northern end of this smaller square. The street is named after hospitals for the poor that could be found, as late as the nineteenth century, in the area of the City Theatre, now the Juliusz Słowacki Theatre, and the gothic św. Krzyż church. Their demolition came with the construction of the theatre, which was built in 1891–95 on the example of the Paris opera by Jan Zawiejski, who was a descendant of the Jewish Feintuch family mentioned earlier.

In the interwar years Szpitalna was one of the city's more characterful streets. It was distinguished by numerous antiquarian bookshops run mainly by Jews. Among them were such eminent and well-known booksellers as the Himmelblaus, the Seidens and the Taffets.

At the beginning of the twentieth century Ahawat Raim's prayer house

Ul. Szpitalna 38, the 'Cyganeria' coffee house, frequented by German officers during the occupation

The plaque at Ul. Szpitalna 38 commemorating the attack of the Jewish Combat Organisation on the 'Cyganeria' cafe

was established in the old house at Ul. Szpitalna 24. In 1947 the building was taken over by the parish of Kraków's Orthodox Church.

At number thirty-eight, opposite the City Theatre, was the 'Cyganeria' [Bohemia] coffee house, which was frequented by German officers during the occupation of 1939–45. On the 22 or 24 of December 1942 it was attacked by the ŻOB, the Jewish Combat Organization, commanded by Jude Lieber. This act is marked by a commemorative plaque set in the wall of the building.

Leaving Ul. Szpitalna we once again cross Rynek Główny to enter Ul. Grodzka, which is part of the King's Way. This runs through the city towards the castle on Wawel Hill and is also a small part of an old trade route connecting Kraków with the salt mines in Wieliczka and Bochnia and, further afield, with Hungary. When we reach the crossroads of Ul. Grodzka with Plac Dominikański on the left and Plac Wszystkich Świętych on the right, we pass two mediaeval churches with their attached monasteries. On the left is the Dominican order and on the right the Franciscan. Next to the Franciscan Church is the former Wielopolski Palace, which is now the seat of the city council. This most recent use of the building is emphasised by the statues there of two distinguished Presidents of Kraków from the second half of the nineteenth century: Józef Dietl and Mikołaj Zyblikiewicz. Just after the crossroads, on the site of numbers twenty-eight and thirty Ul. Grodzka, there was, in the interwar years, another city-centre prayer house. It was funded by Mordechaj Tigner and was erected in 1913 and then rebuilt in 1931 by the architects Isaac Goldberg and Israel Messinger. After the Second World War it was used for a time by the Musical Theatre before lying abandoned and neglected and, finally, falling into irreversible ruin.

Moving further down Ul. Grodzka we reach the next churches. There is the baroque church of St Peter and Paul, the Romanesque church of St Andrew, and St Martin's, which belongs to the Augsberg Evangelical parish. A number of Kraków Jews who decided to assimilate thoroughly and adopt the Christian faith joined this congregation.

At number sixty-two in the years 1879-1939 there was a Hebrew printing press which was run until 1914 by Józef Fiszer, 'The glory years of this printing

The remains of the Mordechai Tigner prayer house, Ul. Grodzka 28/30

press were the 1890s when Fiszer started, at his own expense, to publish the journal 'Hazman' edited by Ruben Aszer Braude from Vilnius. When the journal ceased publication in 1892 Fiszer summoned the editor of 'Hamagidu', I. Sz. Fuchs, from Berlin, and continued to publish 'Hazman' with his own resources from 1892-1903. The reputation of this printing press had soon spread throughout the world so that, with the difficulties caused by censorship in Russia and in the Congress Kingdom, Hebrew journals began to be published by Fiszer in Kraków. The famous Jewish philosopher Achad Haam (Aszer Ginzburg) made an extended stay to print his monthly 'Hasziloach' with Fiszer. Perec often dropped in to Kraków to keep an eye on the monthlies he published. Chaim Nachman Bialik spent a long time here, Friszman printed his works here and Mendele Mocher Sforim, Rawnicki, Szolem Alejchem and Szalom Asz, and many other Jewish and Hebrew men of letters, came to Fiszer for longer or shorter periods to work. In time, all the Hebrew publishing houses moved to Fiszer: Achiasaf and Tuszija from Warsaw and Moria from Odessa. The Warsaw preacher Isaac Cylkow printed his superb translation of the Bible into Polish at Fiszer's press. With Fiszer's death and the outbreak of war in 1914 this golden, blessed period came to an end' (Bałaban, *Przewodnik*, pp. 25–6).

In the part of the defensive wall which surrounded old Kraków and that corresponds with the end of the present Ul. Grodzka was the goldsmiths' gate, which was also used by Jews walking from Kazimierz to Rynek Główny. Beyond the defensive wall lay the settlement of Stradom. As we stand there now, looking from the small church of St Idzi, which was first erected in the eleventh century and then reconstructed in the fourteenth, a view of the eastern wall of the King's Castle on Wawel Hill lies before us.

From at least as early as the eighth century there was a defensive castle of the Vistulanian tribe on Wawel Hill, while from the tenth century it was a seat of Princes and, from the year 1000, the permanent seat of the Kraków Bishops. From the eleventh century there began to be built a set of defensive sacred and secular stone buildings. This was developed gradually in the Gothic period of the fourteenth century and in the sixteenth century Renaissance, before being reconstructed in the Baroque period. The castle was seriously damaged during the Swedish occupation of 1655–57, the Austrian partition (until 1911 sheep were kept there) and the German occupation of 1939-45, when it became the headquarters of the head of the General Gouvernement, Hans Frank. During this period the Royal stables and kitchen were thrown into disorder, Kazimierz the Great's gothic apartments served as a pub and the Senators' Hall was equipped as a cinema. Many artworks were sent to the Reich. The castle was restored after the Second World War and the museum established there, as well as the other historical buildings and monuments on Wawel Hill, are visited each year by thousands of people from Poland and throughout the world.

We cannot move on from Wawel without devoting a few words to the most outstanding of Poland's rulers, Kazimierz the Great (1333-70). While he was on the throne Poland was united and thrust onto the path of rapid growth and development. The King, seeing Jews as useful immigrants, who could help the cities and the economy grow, awarded them extensive privileges in 1364 and 1367 and because of this they always had fond memories of him. There are many accurate and inaccurate tales in circulation about all distinguished people and Kazimierz the Great is no exception. One tells of his love for the beautiful Ester, the daughter of a Jewish tailor from Opoczno. The King so cherished her that, apart from a daughter whose name we do not know, she bore him two sons: Niemir and Pełko. Kazimierz had no sons from any of his legal marriages.

The daughter remained with the mother and was brought up a Jew. The sons, though, were taken care of by the King and grew up as Christians. The King is supposed to have built Ester a palace in Łobzów outside Kraków but the castles in Niepołomice and Bochotnica are also mentioned in this context. There is also the suggestion that Ester's house was in Kazimierz at Ul. Krakowska 46, and that there was an underground link between there and Wawel. The tale persists, in material form, in the name of Kazimierz's Ul. Estery.

For Jews Wawel was pre-eminent. After all, they were not subject to the city authorities, but to the King, who protected them, took care of them and levied taxes from them. Although the King exercised power over the Jews indirectly through voivodes, in important matters, such as the conferral or confir-

Home of the legendary Ester, Ul. Krakowska 46,
now the Ethnographic Museum

mation of privileges and in questions and events requiring immediate intervention, Jewish delegations had direct recourse to the King at Wawel.

From Wawel we make our way to Ul. Stradom and are immediately confronted by two churches: the Bernardyne church of St Agnieszka's (1680) on the right and the Missionary church of St Paul's on the left.

Until 1800 Stradom was administratively separate from Kraków. From 1815–46, when Kraków was known as the Free City of Kraków, only assimilated Jews, or those willing to assimilate, could settle there. Over the course of the second half of the nineteenth century the number of Jews living in Stradom grew relatively quickly. Solomon Deiches, vice-president of the Jewish Denominational Council, had a house at number eighteen, while the Gumplowicz family had a house at number twenty-two. Abraham

Gumplowicz was one of the most active advocates of the assimilation and polonisation of Kraków's Jews. His son, Ludwik (1838-1909), attempted to become an assistant professor at the Jagiellonian University with a thesis on the legal context and position of the Polish Jews. It was not accepted though, and Ludwik moved to Austria where he excelled as a Sociologist and went on to become professor at Graz University. Marcin Feintuch lived at the last house in the street, number twenty-six. He was a descendant of the Zawiejski family and of the Szarski family who owned the 'grey' tenement on Rynek Główny. By the interwar period Stradom was almost entirely Jewish and, first of all, a trading area. In the 1930s at number ten was the Secondary Commercial School, whose director was the philologist, journalist and Zionist activist, Samuel Stendig. He was murdered in Lwów in 1942.

Ul. Stradom ends at the crossroads with Ul. Dietla, which was built on the filled-in bed of the old Wisła river in 1878-80. It takes its name from Dr. Józef Dietl, who was an outstanding President of Kraków (1866-75). In those days Ul. Dietla, with its broad, green strip flanked by two carriageways – the tramlines did not come until 1969 – represented a new departure in urban planning. It also made the area healthier to live in and this set off a burst in new building with the Jews to the fore as investors, as the owners of building companies and as architects. Soon, the Jews had occupied almost all the land in this new area which, when compared to the pinched passages and alleys of old Kazimierz, could be described without exaggeration as a 'New World'. Apart from comfortable residential homes Ul. Dietla also saw the development of important social institutions. For example, a new Jewish orphanage was built at number sixty-four in 1872-5. It was extended significantly after the First World War with the help of Kraków Jews living and working abroad. The driving force behind this was Róża Rockowa, who was head of the *Bet Megadle Jesomim* Association for the Care of Jewish Orphans in Kraków. In 1937 there were eighty-nine orphans of both sexes in the orphanage and nineteen girls were cared for and educated in the Apprentices' hostel for girls the Association maintained.

In the interwar years the Jews became considerably more active in sport, and a number of clubs, such as Makkabi, Jutrzenka and Hagibor, were established. Of these, the strongest was

Makkabi, which was established in 1909 and was very successful at soccer and athletics, and particularly so at water polo with its team competing with the best for the Polish championship. The club had a stadium on Ul. Dietla near Wawel Castle, which is now used by the Nadwiślan club, and a rowing station on the river nearby.

Crossing Ul. Dietla at the crossroads with Ul. Stradom and Ul. Krakowska we enter Kazimierz.

Remembering what we have already said about the old Wisła river it will be easier to understand that Kazimierz was, in effect, an island sitting in the waters flowing in the main channel of the Wisła and its older tributary. This area was already settled in the early middle-ages. In 1335 Kazimierz the Great founded a new town here and gave it his name. In 1340 it expanded to take in an area donated by the King that was once part of the village of Bawół. In the fourteenth century the town was encircled with a defensive wall with four gates. To the north was the Kraków gate, to the south the Wieliczka and Bocheńska gates and to the west the Skawina gate. The keystones of Kazimierz's economy were trade and crafts – especially the making of woollen cloth. The biggest trading place was the main market square, which measured 188m x 141m. It had a brick-built town hall, a weigh station and a cloth hall similar to the one in Kraków's Rynek Główny. In the north-east corner of the square the Parish Church of Corpus Christi was built. It was paid for by Kazimierz the Great and begun in 1340. It was completed in the middle of the following century by the Lutheran Canons Regular, who were brought to Kazimierz by Władysław Jagiełło in 1405. A second important place of worship in Kazimierz, Skałka, which was founded by Kazimierz the Great for the Augustinian Order, began to be built in the second half of the fourteenth century. This is Kazimierz's oldest settled site and it became an extremely important place of worship. The first church here was erected very early, and it was here, in 1079, that the Bishop of Kraków, Stanisław of Szczepanów, was killed by King Bolesław the Bold. The cult of the murdered Bishop had an enormous influence on the fate and fortune of the Pauline Church and Monastery that was established on the site in 1472.

שרה שנירר ע״ה
נפטרה כ״ו אדר תרצ״ה

...אשה אם לאלפים ורבבות   ...זכרונות הערצה נאמנים
אם מלטפת ומוכיחה   ילוו את נשמתה הגדולה
בלהט דבריה נשבו לבבות   ימשך מאות דורות ושנים
להט אם אוהבת ומשגיחה...   יזכר שמה בכבוד ותהלה.

ל׳ אלכסנדר זושא פרידמן הי״ד

THIS BUILDING, BUILT AND DEDICATED IN 1927, WAS THE
HOME OF THE BETH JACOB TEACHERS' SEMINARY FOUNDED IN
1917 BY SARAH SCHENIRER. IT WAS HERE THAT DAUGHTERS OF
ISRAEL, FROM MANY CORNERS OF CENTRAL AND EASTERN
EUROPE, CAME TO STUDY TORAH.
A SPARK KINDLED IN KRAKOW GREW TO A FLAME THAT
RADIATED THROUGHOUT POLAND AND ACROSS THE OCEANS. THIS
LIGHT OF TORAH CONTINUES TO ILLUMINATE THE HEARTS AND
MINDS OF JEWISH GIRLS THROUGHOUT THE WORLD.

W BUDYNKU TYM MIEŚCIŁA SIĘ ŻEŃSKA SZKOŁA BET JAKOW,
ZAŁOŻONA PRZEZ SARĘ SCHENIRER W ROKU 1917. BUDYNEK
WYBUDOWANY W 1927 ROKU BYŁ MIEJSCEM DLA DZIEWCZĄT
ŻYDOWSKICH, KTÓRE PRZYJEŻDŻAŁY Z RÓŻNYCH STRON
ŚWIATA, ABY STUDIOWAĆ TORĘ.

REDEDICATED BY THE SARAH SCHENIRER COMMEMORATIVE COMMITTEE
AGUDAH WOMEN OF AMERICA
MAY 2001 אייר תשס״א

The plaque commemorating the former Bejt Jakow girls' school
at Ul. Świętego Stanisława 10

Now we are on this side of Ul. Dietla we should have a brief look at two of its side streets: Orzeszkowa and św. Stanisław. In the interwar years *'Nowy Dziennik'* [The New Daily], the newspaper most widely read by Kraków Jews, was printed and edited at Ul. Orzeszkowej 7. In the five-storey building at Ul. św. Stanisława 10, built in 1928-33 to the design of Samuel Singer, was a seminary dedicated to training female teachers for the *Bejt Jakow* schools. The first school of this type in Kraków was established on the initiative of Sara Szenirer (1883-1935) in 1917. Her great concern was to raise and educate girls in the spirit of the Jewish religion and in this way to counter the tendency to assimilation. She was also devoted to closing the educational gap between the women and men from this religious background. Both the schools and the teachers' seminary met with great success and in 1937 there were around 120 girls studying at the seminary. By the same year the

Bejt Jakow network of schools had expanded to more than 250 institutions, with a combined total of 40,000 female students, distributed between Poland, other European countries, and the USA and Palestine. In Poland this dynamic growth was possible thanks to the support given the schools by members of the Orthodox *Agudat Yisrael* movement and, especially, senator Mojżesz Deutscher (1878-1941), who was the mainstay of the Kraków headquarters and of all of the major *Bejt Jakow* institutions.

From Ul. św. Stanisława we return to Ul. Krakowska, which is the main street on this route.

The Jews, who were certainly already present in Kazimierz in the fourteenth century, and who came there in significant numbers at the end of the fifteenth century, used to occupy only a fifth of the town. Jewish economic activity in Christian Kazimierz developed on a large scale only after 1776 when they lost the battle for the right to trade in Kraków with the city's Guild of Merchants. From 1816 the Jews could settle freely anywhere in Kazimierz

The former Süsser family home, Ul. Krakowska 13, circa 1900

and, gradually, through the nineteenth century and into the early decades of the twentieth, the town assumed its identity as the Jewish district of Kraków. So, as we move along Ul. Krakowska in the direction of Plac Wolnica, we are passing houses that were bought, rather than built, by the Jews. One of the more imposing of them is number thirteen. It took its present form at the end of the eighteenth century when two houses were joined to form a magnifi-cent, Baroque classical palace. Then, it was owned by the nobleman, Andrzej Wolf, but by the end of the nineteenth century it had passed into the hands of the Jewish Süsser family.

We now reach Plac Wolnica, which was Kazimierz's equivalent of Kraków's Rynek Główny and was once almost as big. Plac Wolnica had a similar design with the town hall in the middle and the Corpus Christi parish church in the north-east corner – just where Kraków's Mariacki

The former Süsser family home, Ul. Krakowska 13

The former Kazimierz town hall in Plac Wolnica, now the Ethnographic Museum

A replica of Henryk Hochmann's bas-relief *The Reception of the Jews* into Poland on the former Kazimierz town hall in Plac Wolnica

church stands in the Rynek Główny. The Kazimierz town hall was built in the fourteenth century. In 1830, when the building was no longer a town hall, it functioned as a state elementary school for Jewish children. On its eastern wall is a replica of Henryk Hochman's (1879-1943) bas-relief *The Reception of the Jews into Poland* which was made by the artist in 1907. It was originally on the northern wall but was removed during the German occupation of 1939-45. A similar fate was met by another of Hochman's bas-reliefs, *Queen Jadwiga*, which adorned the interior of the Jewish Council House on Ul. Krakowska.

Headquarters of the Jewish Denominational Council on the corner of Ul. Krakowska and Ul. Skawińska

The Reception of the Jews into Poland was stored in the National Museum in Warsaw and returned to the wall of the Town Hall in 1996 on the occasion of the visit to Kraków of Ehud Olmert, then the Mayor of Jerusalem and later Prime Minister of Israel.

We find the Jewish council house near to the corner of Ul. Krakowska (number forty-five) and Ul. Skawińska (number two) which, if we imagine a line extending it across Ul. Krakowska, forms the old southern side of the market square. The council house was built in 1911 and designed by Herman Lamensdorf. In the interwar years it was shared by a number of other institutions. On the ground floor was the 'Ezra'

Judaic library, which had been established in 1899 by a group of 'progressives' including Leon Horowitz, the then head of the council, Herman Hirsch, Ozjasz Thon, Zygmunt Klein, Juliusz Schönwetter and many others. During the Second World War the collection was broken down and dispersed. The Jewish council office was on the first floor, with

in the middle-ages by Jews taking refuge from persecution in Germany. It disappeared during the Second World War and, after a time, reappeared in a German library. From there, it joined the collection of the National Library in the University of Jerusalem.

The Jewish Denominational Council still has its headquarters in the

The Jewish Hospital at Ul. Skawińska 8 then (circa 1890)

the council chamber and archive on the second. Its most important holding was, perhaps, an illuminated manuscript of the Hebrew Bible from the fourteenth century, which probably came from Regensburg. It was brought to Kraków

building. Apart from the council office there is a kitchen and canteen providing kosher food to the community.

Further along Ul. Skawińska at number eight there was a Jewish hospital from 1822-1939. The more recent building, whose *spiritus rector* was Dr Józef Oettinger, was erected in 1861-6 and designed by Antoni Stacherski, but it expanded and developed most intensively during the inter-war years, when its director and head of paediatrics was Dr Jan Landau (1871-1936). Because the members of the Jewish community in Kraków used the hospital services free of charge it would not have been possible to maintain and develop it without the additional money raised by the Society of Friends of the Jewish Hospital, which was established on Landau's initiative in 1933. New departments were added, including outpatients and other clinics, and up-to-date equipment was acquired. The hospital also had outstanding medical staff. Among them were the internal specialists Maksymilian Blassberg and Julian Aleksandrowícz, the laryngologist Adolf Schwarzbart, who published many articles in leading medical journals, the radiologist Marcel Spitzer, who wrote a work about cancer that was awarded the Józef Piłsudski prize, the neurologist Bernard Bornstein and the ophthalmologist Edmund Rosenhauch. In the 1930s the hospital treated more than 2,000 patients every year, while 20,000 every year took advantage of the outpatient facilities. During the Second World War most of the staff continued to work in the Podgórze ghetto and the Płaszów concentration camp. Since the end of the war the building has been used by the local health service.

Not far from this building at Ul. Wietora 7, in a house built in 1936, was the Ognisko Pracy school. This was a

▼ .... and now

vocational secondary school for girls, which taught shirt-making, dressmaking, knitting and home economics, as well as the subjects compulsory in all state schools. The director, Eliza Fraenkel, who was active on the council for a long period, made a great contribution to its growth and development.

Leaving Ul. Skawińska we return to Plac Wolnica and reach the street that forms its southern side, Ul. Bocheńska. Here, at number four, in a house built just before the First World War by Henryk Lamensdorf, was the Sherit Bne Emuna prayer house. It stood empty for many years after the end of the Second World War before being adapted in the 1990s for use by the health service and as a teaching facility of the Jagiellonian University's Medical College.

Another notable place on Ul. Bocheńska is the building at number seven which, from 1926, was the permanent home of the Jewish Theatre. That it was established was due in large measure to the Kraków Bund activists and lovers of Jewish theatre Mojżesz Kanfer, Abraham Seidenfeld, Fryderyk Freund and Maurycy Fiszer. There were also two Jewish poets: Mordechaj

Gebirtig and Ber Horowitz. The play presented at the theatre's inauguration on 13 October 1926, which was written in the same year, was Altera Kaczyne's *'Dukus'* [The Duke], a drama based on the Jewish tradition of the 'righteous proselyte' – the Polish Count, Walentyn Potocki. It was directed by Jonasz Turkow, a famous actor from Warsaw. In those years many superb actors, including Ida Kamińska, the Turkows, Szymon Dżygan and Izrael Schumacher, made guest appearances, and there were also visits from the best theatre groups. The Vilnius company, for example, played *'Dybuka'* [The Dibbuk] and *'Dzień i noc'* [Night and Day] by An-Ski, as well as *'Zazdrość'* [Jealousy] by Arcybashev. The theatre also had its own company of actors and, thanks to this, could draw on the rich reserves of Jewish literature to amuse and stir its audience.

After the Second World War the stage on Bocheńska was taken over by the amateur group Teatr Kolejarza [The Railway Workers' Theatre]. Its closure in the late 1980s ended the theatrical phase in the history of number seven.

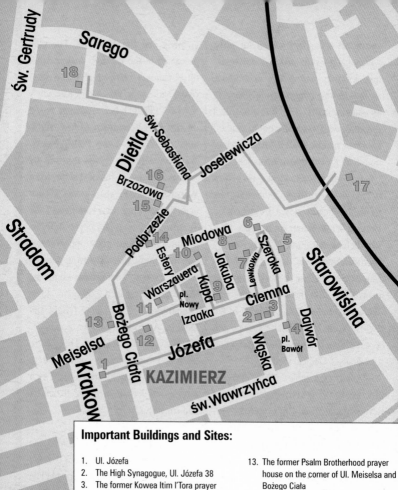

Important Buildings and Sites:

1. Ul. Józefa
2. The High Synagogue, Ul. Józefa 38
3. The former Kowea Itim l'Tora prayer house, Ul. Józefa 42
4. The Old Synagogue
5. The Popper Synagogue
6. The Ritual Baths (mykwa). Ul. Szeroka 6
7. The Remu Synagogue
8. The Old Cemetery
9. The Izaak Synagogue
10. The Kupa Synagogue
11. Plac Nowy
12. Center for Jewish Culture
13. The former Psalm Brotherhood prayer house on the corner of Ul. Meiselsa and Bożego Ciała
14. The Tempel (Progressive) Synagogue
15. The former Hebrew Secondary School on the corner of Ul. Podbrzezie and Brzozowa
16. The former Salomon Deiches prayer house, Ul. Brzozowa 6
17. The New Cemetery
18. Ozjasz Thon's house, Ul. Bogusławskiego 5

ROUTE 2:

ULICA JÓZEFA –
ULICA PRZEMYSKA

▲ A view of Kazimierz from the east circa 1870. To the left Corpus Christi church and to the right part of the Jewish town with the Old Synagogue

Ulica Józefa was the main road connecting Jewish and Christian Kazimierz and was named to commemorate a visit made by the Austrian Emperor Joseph II. Much earlier it had been called Ul. Sukiennicza and, before taking the Emperor's name, Ul. Żydowska. Its first section, between Ul. Krakowska and the crossroads with Ul. Bożego Ciała, was not part of the Jewish town, which began only after the crossroads. It must be pointed out, though, that this was the case only from the seventeenth century. It was then that the area to the north of Ul. Józefa, from Ul. Jakuba to Ul. Bożego Ciała, was added to the Jewish town.

Ulica Józefa in the 1930s

Ul. Józefa has retained much of its old, slightly sleepy small town atmosphere. The ground floors are still occupied by shops, but their business has changed. Gone are the majority of grocery shops and small craft workshops. In their place are art galleries, junk and curiosity shops, antique shops, cafes and hotels.

On the right hand side of Ul. Józefa at numbers nine and eleven are the old monastery buildings which housed the parish school run by the Corpus Christi monks. In the sixteenth and seventeenth centuries Jews passing this way to the Christian town and Kraków had to pay a toll to do so and were also forced to pay the pupils a fee on a basket of goods

▲ The yard between Ul. Józefa and Ul. Rabbi Meiselsa, 1916

Jewish children on the corner of Ul. Bożego Ciała and Św. Wawrzyńca in 1930

33

Ul. Józefa

known as a *kozubalec*. This often led to noisy arguments.

The Jewish town proper began where Ul. Józefa and Ul. Jakuba intersect today. As late as the end of the nineteenth century a renaissance house built in 1536 by Giovanni Cini of Sienna and Filipe of Fiesole for Jonasz, son of Abraham, was still standing at today's Ul. Jakuba 36. At the turn of the sixteenth and seventeenth centuries it belonged to the wealthy Jew, Feliks, and from 1790 to Eliasz Herslowicz. All the owners were obliged to make over a certain proportion of proceeds of any sale or rental transactions to maintain the eternal flame in the High Synagogue. Among the various people who lived there at the turn of the eighteenth and nineteenth centuries it is worth mentioning Lipman Krengel, the grandfather of Emanuel Krengel, who later became a rabbinical judge and wrote a biographical dictionary of well-known Jews

Ul. Józefa with the High Synagogue, circa 1919

called *Szem Ha-gedolim Haszalem*. Around 1884 the house was abandoned and pulled down. Several years later a new, three-storey house was put up on the site and it is still there today.

The gates of the Jewish town were almost level with the house at number thirty-six. They were guarded day and night and all those entering were stopped, 'The guards may have had a difficult job (...) but the Jewish Council had problems with *them,* because they fleeced Jewish merchants they didn't know and, more than that, they barred the way to wedding parties and extracted heavy fees to allow the bridegroom, best man, bridesmaids and family into the city. To prevent this, the Kahal, in

a statute of 1595, set a fixed tax that the guards were obliged to collect on the day after a wedding from a bridegroom from another town' (Bałaban, *Przewodnik*, pp. 33–4).

The High Synagogue

This, one of the oldest of the synagogues, was erected behind the town gates. It stands amongst the densely juxtaposed buildings of Ul. Józefa at number thirty-eight. Built in the shape of a rectangle, it faces the street with its shorter, southern elevation supported by four buttresses. Between them, at the level of the third floor, are the three

The High Synagogue, Ul. Józefa 38

high, arched windows of the men's prayer room.

After the Old and New (Remu) Synagogues, the High Synagogue was the third to be built in the Jewish town. It was constructed after 1556, but no later than 1563, next to the rich Jew Feliks's house, referred to earlier, on the corner of Ul. Józefa and Ul. Jakuba. At that time these streets marked the southern and western border of the Jewish district of Kazimierz, whose main gate was at their intersection. The High Synagogue is so called because its prayer room was well above ground level. This untypical arrangement was dictated by safety concerns. The synagogue was close to the town gate which was a very busy place, full of the noises of the street and also, at that time, in close proximity to the Christian town. The entrance to the synagogue led through a hallway in the western, narrower part of the building on the first floor. From almost the moment the synagogue was completed there were probably shops in its eastern, wider section, and this was also to be the case in later periods.

Until the middle of the seventeenth century there was only the original body of the building in the shape of a rectangle. The high, open men's prayer room occupying the first and second floors once featured a cradle vault. Light was admitted by three windows arranged symmetrically on both the southern and eastern sides. One of its original architectural details, a fragment of which has been preserved, is the stone altar cupboard in the eastern wall. While its layout and interior does not differ from that of other Kraków synagogues, its door is extremely interesting. It was made at the beginning of the seventeenth century by Solomon and Chaim, who were sons of Aron, and is a two-leafed door decorated on its outer side with a relief image of the Polish eagle. On its inner side are images of ceremonial objects: a menorah (seven-stemmed candela-

Interior of the High Synagogue

brum) and a table with sacrificial loaves of bread. Evidence of the prayer room's seventeenth century interior can be found in the remnants of murals featuring prayer texts. These were discovered and restored in the 1960s.

In the second half of the seventeenth century an annex was built next to the synagogue's northern wall with a women's prayer house on its first floor. The building adjacent on the western side, number thirty-six, was used to further extend the synagogue. At the end of the 1880s on its first floor two prayer houses were established – to the north for the men and to the south for the women. The buildings were connected by openings made in the High Synagogue's western wall. A prayer room for the Ner Tamid brotherhood was established on the ground floor.

The synagogue's structure deteriorated between 1939–51 and its furnishings, including precious examples of ceremonial art, were entirely lost. In 1951 a design was produced to adapt the synagogue and the two-storey house on its eastern side, number forty, for use by one of Kraków's theatres. By this time the northern women's prayer room no longer existed, and there were plans for a terrace to be built in its place. Although the former synagogue was never occupied by a theatre, the general idea of joining it with the house on its eastern side was followed through in 1966, when both structures were converted and adapted for the Kraków section of the Historic Monuments Preservation Studio. The men's prayer room was covered with a flat ceiling to replace the destroyed cradle vault and a new door opening connecting the prayer room to the first floor of the neighboring building was made opposite the altar cupboard. Also, the ancient, stone alms-box from the western wall of the men's prayer room was placed on the landing of the staircase at number forty. During renovation work on the men's prayer room fragments of seventeenth century murals were exposed, while in the western wall the recesses remain of the now bricked-up arcades of the women's prayer room, and of the door opening in the men's. The building was covered with a new ridge roof with broad eaves, while the southern and northern gables were glazed to provide extra light for the technical workshops in the attic. At the end of the 1990s the Historical Monuments Preservation Studio left the former synagogue.

A further structure to enjoy on Ul. Józefa is the single-storey house at number forty-two which, from the beginning of the nineteenth century, was

The Old Synagogue from Ul. Józefa in the 1930s

the Kowea Itim l'Tora prayer house, whose name denotes those who regularly study the Torah. On the facade we can see the Hebrew name of the prayer house and, within two stars of David, the dates in Hebrew of its establishment (1810) and restoration (1912). It is now a residential building.

The odd-numbered houses where Ul. Józefa meets the Old Synagogue were built in the 1990s on the site of old houses that were run down to ruin and finally demolished after prolonged agonies endured 'playing' the role of the burning town of Kaliniec, with the agreement of the City Conservation

Officer, in the feature film 'Noce i Dnie' [Nights and Days] shot in Kazimierz in 1976. The ruins of the oldest Hassidic prayer house in the old town, *Reb Arons Klaus*, which was founded in 1815 by Kalman Epstein and later named after his eldest son Aron, and which stood at Ul. Józefa 33, also went up in flames during the location filming.

Where Ul. Józefa meets the Old Synagogue we turn left into Ul. Szeroka,

The former Kowea Itim I' Tora prayer house, ul. Józefa 42

which is a spacious square enclosed at its shortest sides by two dominant buildings: the Old Synagogue on the south side and a three-storey renaissance house with a high, ridge roof on the north side. The longer sides of the square are built up with a series of compact buildings. The exception is the western side leading out to Ul. Miodowa, where we find part of the stone wall enclosing the New (Remu) Synagogue and the old Jewish cemetery. Before the eighteenth century, Ul. Szeroka was called Wielka Ulica and was the focal point of the Jewish town over its lifetime from the fifteenth to the nineteenth century. In a later period, and as late as the first few years after the Second World War, it was one of the busiest junk markets in Kraków. During the 1990s the street changed its old religious and residential character and gradually became the local centre for cafes and hotels that cater for the tourism stimulated by the district's Jewish past.

The most precious Jewish historical buildings and monuments are on Ul. Szeroka: the New (Remu) Synagogue with the Old Cemetery, and the Old Synagogue, which is now a museum of Jewish culture. We shall visit the Old Synagogue first.

The Old Synagogue

The Old Synagogue

This is the oldest of the preserved synagogues in Poland. Although its architecture was shaped in the renaissance, it has a clear connection with the Gothic as it compares with the double-naved synagogues built earlier in the eleventh century in Worms, in the twelfth century in Regensburg, in the thirteenth and fourteenth centuries in Prague, in Eger in 1375 and in Oleśnica in Śląsk in the fourteenth century. The original synagogue was probably built here at the beginning of the fifteenth century (1407?) and was the first in Kazimierz. The eastern wall was built against the town's defensive wall. At that time it was exclusively for men. It had a rectangular, double-naved hall with a crossed rib vault resting on two pillars and was covered by a ridge roof. The hall floor was below street level, which was necessary if the building was to be entirely screened by the fortifications. In the second half of the sixteenth century two single-floor additions were made with a vestibule at the north-western corner and a women's prayer room behind the vestibule against the hall's western wall.

41

The Old Synagogue from Plac Bawół

In time, a Kahal house was added and with this the Old Synagogue became the religious and administrative centre of Kraków's Jewish community.

In 1570 the gothic synagogue was rebuilt by Mateusz Gucci – one of a large number of Italian architects and builders then in Kraków. He raised the walls to their present height and, unusually for the time, restored the hall's vaulting to its original crossed rib form resting on two slim Tuscan columns. A new wrought iron canopy-shaped bimah was placed on a dodecagonal stone plinth between them, and the prayer room walls were decorated with murlas with a grapevine motif. The exterior of the building saw many changes.

The raised hall walls with the prolate, arched windows were topped with an arcaded attic that concealed the sunken roof behind it.

At the end of the sixteenth century and in the first half of the seventeenth further women's prayer rooms were added to the main hall at its southern and northern sides. The synagogue was next reshaped at the end of the nineteenth century and in the early decades of the twentieth. In 1889 the main roof was rebuilt and in 1891 Jan Sas-Zubrzycki restored the western facade, which was exposed after the old Kahal house had been demolished. Extensive restoration work was carried out by Zygmunt Hendel in 1904, 1913

The interior of the museum at the Old Synagogue

and 1923. This enhanced the building's technical and functional standards and, with the addition of neo-renaissance details, enriched its architecture. A second storey was added to the outhouse at the north-western corner and the surrounding land was brought down to its sixteenth century level and enclosed with an ornamental fence. In addition, a small museum was established in the new rooms where the synagogue's antique religious objects and documents were kept until 1939.

During the Second World War the synagogue was taken over by the German Trust Office and its interior furnishings were destroyed. It was then used as a storeroom. Not long after – the date cannot be reliably established – the synagogue's storeroom was liquidated and its vault destroyed – probably deliberately. The synagogue remained in ruins for more than a decade after the war. It was rebuilt in 1956–59 and handed over to the City of Kraków Historical Museum by the Jewish Denominational Council with the right of perpetual usufruct. The Museum established a permanent collection reflecting the culture and history of the Kraków Jews and

The Old Synagogue in the 1920s. In the background to the rights is Ul. Szeroka

now organizes exhibitions presenting all aspects of the history and culture of the Jews in Poland.

But the Old Synagogue's history would be far from complete if it were told only in architectural terms. After all, it was exceptional among the Kazimierz synagogues. First of all, it was the oldest of the Jewish Community's prayer houses and so naturally became its most important. But as well as being a centre of religious life it was a seat of authority for the Jewish town's Rabbis and Elders, 'It was here that the most important citizens, primarily the Rabbis and Kraków Rectors, prayed. Marriages were celebrated in the courtyard and from the almemar the ordinances of Kings, voivodes and Kahal Elders were read and recalcitrant citizens were excommunicated. Here the community assembled in good times and bad and offered up their prayers when plague loomed or when a drought threatened bad crops and hunger. Here, in July 1616 a rare summer prayer for rain, 'Wa-ten tal u-matar li-wracha' was repeated for eight consecutive days with another prayer for rain following in 1621.' (Bałaban, *Historia* I, p. 411). In 1794 Tadeusz Kościuszko spoke from the bimah to encourage the Jews to lend their active support to the insurrection of that year. Patriotic speeches to the Jews were also delivered here by Maurycy Krzepicki, a member of the local Jewish Committee (1846), during the Kraków Uprising, and by Ber Meisels, a famous Kraków Rabbi (1848), during the Springtime of Nations.

Growing interest in history and architectural monuments spurred people from way beyond the Kraków Jewish community to visit the Old Synagogue. In 1887, for example, the Austrian Archduke Rudolf and his wife Stefania came.

The tradition of important people visiting the Old Synagogue continued into the twentieth century in independent Poland when Kraków's Jews received the Republic's President, Ignacy Mościcki, in 1927.

There are a profusion of folk tales concerning the Old Synagogue. According to one, permission to build the synagogue was granted the Jews by Kazimierz the Great, who donated swords decorated with angels' heads

Chief Rabbi J.N. Kornitzer and representatives of the Jewish Community awaiting the visit of President Ignacy Mościcki before the Old Synagogue, 1927

to be melted and cast into chandeliers. Though it was against the Torah, which forbids figurative images and 'false idols' in a synagogue, the Jews hung the swords there for some time to show their gratitude, and so that the monarch would not be offended.

One of the Old Synagogue's particular traditions was the original Simhat Torah holiday ceremony. Usually, this holiday culminates in joyful dancing with the Torah scrolls, which are carried seven times around the bimah. But in the Old Synagogue the tradition was different because of an event which, though unconfirmed, probably really did take place in the years of unrest after the wars with Sweden in the second half of the seventeenth century. On Simhat Torah, when all the Jews were gathered in the synagogue, some Kraków university students forced their way into the Jewish town under cover of darkness. They made an assault on the Old Synagogue at exactly the moment the Jews were rounding the bimah with the sacred scrolls for the fourth time. They stopped and hastily passed the scrolls from hand to hand to hide them in the ark. Some of the Jews were killed in the tumult caused by the attack. From then on, to commemorate the tragic event, the Simhat Torah dances in the Old Synagogue were interrupted halfway through the fourth circuit when the participants sat down on the overturned benches and, as during the period of fasting and remembering called Tiszabe-aw, said prayers of mourning before resuming the fourth lap.

Ul. Szeroka

After leaving the Old Synagogue we should have a look at the area around it. In the courtyard there is a marble statue that commemorates thirty Poles who were executed here by Germans in 1943. At the north-east corner of the synagogue we can see a reconstructed fragment of the town's defensive wall. One can thus imagine how the Old Synagogue stood in the layout of the mediaeval town. It is likely that the oldest Jewish cemetery in Kazimierz lay behind that wall. But no traces of it remain. There are also no remaining traces of the build-ings that were once between the Old Synagogue and the house at number twenty-two. Here, for example, was the Auf'n Bergel prayer house, which was founded by Mojżesz Jekeles for his son in law, Natan Spira (1583-1633). Spira was a noted Kabbalist and the author of *Megale Amukot* (Disclosures). It is certain that he was an outstanding scholar as the council made him Rector of the local Rabbinical College (rosz metiwta), which post he occupied from 1617 until his death.

From in front of the Old Synagogue we begin a short walk around Ul.

Ul. Szeroka in 1987

47

Szeroka following first the houses on its right, or eastern, side. Even though most of these houses have been here a relatively short time they embody a lineage extending for many hundreds of years. The first three were built in the 1980s and 90s, where houses completely ruined in the post-war period had been. The house that used to stand on the site of today's number eighteen was known as the 'Rabbinical'. Rabbi Izaak Lewita, the Chief Rabbi and Rector of the Rabbinical School, lived there from 1776–79, while his son, Hirsz Dawid Lewita, who was also Chief Rabbi, lived there from 1816–32. Both were entrenched opponents of Hassidism and the father had occasion to twice excommunicate Hassidic Jews, which he did in the Old Synagogue in 1786 and 1797.

We now pass number seventeen, which dates from the sixteenth century and was where the Rabbi of the Wolf Popper (Bocian) Synagogue lived, and come to number sixteen, where, set back from Ul. Szeroka, we find the synagogue itself.

The Wolf Popper (Bocian) Synagogue

The synagogue's eastern facade and the two high windows set deep in it are probably best viewed from Ul. Dajwór, as the view from Ul. Szeroka is obscured by the building's long, gated courtyard. It was built in 1620 by Wolf Popper, who was among the richest Jewish financiers and merchants in Kraków. Because it was not very big it was colloquially known as the Small Synagogue. On its eastern side it used to adjoin the town's defensive wall. In the nineteenth century, along its northern and western walls, a pair of two-storey extensions were built, which were used as women's

The gates of the Wolf Popper Synagogue

The Wolf Popper Synagogue

prayer houses. On the ground floor of the western extension there was a vestibule for the men's prayer room. Next to this was a smaller, two-storey outhouse that served as the synagogue's office. At the end of the nineteenth century it was fairly extensively restored. It was then that its roof, as well as the stairs and connecting porch for the first-floor women's galleries, was built. During the same restoration works a triaxial, brick gate closing the courtyard from the Ul. Szeroka side was also erected.

There is very little information about the objects and interior of the Popper Synagogue. The interwar guidebooks mention the oak door to the altar niche, which was polychrome and deco-rated with bas-reliefs depicting a lion, an eagle, a deer and a leopard to symbolise the strengths and abilities of man following in the steps of God and aspiring to God's perfection. This is now in the collection of the Wolfson Museum in Jerusalem. The same guidebooks describe period murals and paintings on the synagogue's vault that were done by Schoenker.

The synagogue's furnishings were either destroyed or lost in the extermination of the Kraków Jews in the Second World War. After the war the building was no longer used as a place of worship, but Jews who came to Kraków from the Soviet Union lived for a few years in its former women's section.

49

Interior of the Wolf Popper Synagogue

What remained of the old synagogue was the main body of the building, the men's room and the northern women's room. In 1965 it was adapted and renovated before being handed over to the central Kraków Cultural Centre for use as an arts studio. With the blessing of the Jewish Denominational Council the arts studio has remained there ever since.

After our visit to the former synagogue at number sixteen we continue our walk around Ul. Szeroka. Helena Rubenstein was born in 1872 in a modest, two-storey house at number fourteen. In 1890 the future 'Queen of Cosmetics' left to join relations in Australia. There, she opened her first cosmetics business and had her first success with her mother's herbal cream brought over from Kraków. It was not long before HR cosmetics stormed the European and American markets.

In the last of the houses on this side of Ul. Szeroka, number six, were the community, or ritual, baths known as mykwa. They were also known as the 'big' baths to distinguish them from the smaller ritual baths which were near to today's Plac Nowy, 'the attendant was supposed to heat the baths at least once every two weeks, and every Friday. In 1806 the baths were leased by Jekele Felczer, known as 'the Doctor', who paid the Kahal treasurer 831 Polish Złoty per annum for the privilege. At that time a ticket cost three grosze. But if the prospective bather was a woman engaged to be married the leaseholder collected a tax proportional to her dowry as the entry fee'. (Bałaban, *Przewodnik*, pp. 656). To reach the baths one had to walk down forty steps as that was the level of the spring feeding them, 'Once the baths had a timber casing, but now there are cement walls and stone steps. Despite this it still reminds us of a mediaeval ritual bath in an old German community like Worms or Friedburg...' (Bałaban, *Przewodnik*, p. 66). The building had been rebuilt so many times that, as early as the interwar years, a Jewish historian was moved to express regret at the lack of respect for the past that had brought the building to its ravaged state. After thorough modernisation and adaptation in 1974–76 the Kraków section of the Historic Monuments Preservation Studio took over the building. In the 1990s ownership of the baths passed to the Jewish Denominational Council and it became one of the many restaurants on this side of Ul. Szeroka. What remains of the baths is preserved in the cellars.

Where there were six houses in the seventeenth century, three houses now form the northern side of Ul. Szeroka. In the seventeenth century the houses belonged to influential members of the Jewish community. Among them was Rabbi Jozue Heszel, who was Chief Rabbi and Rector of the Rabbinical School in 1654-63. There was also Samuel Kac, a doctor from Padua, who for many years during the first half of the seventeenth century was an Elder of the Kazimierz Kahal. In the eighteenth century three of the houses were joined together to provide a home for several families. From the nineteenth century the most prominent owners were the exceptionally prolific and well-connected Landau family. Among them was Dr Rafał Landau, a lawyer, who was the last President of Kraków's Jewish Council.

A leafy garden enclosed with decorative iron work takes up a part of the northern section of Ul. Szeroka. At its southern end there is a memorial to Holocaust victims who came from in and around Kraków. Before 1552, when the nearby cemetery of the New (Remu) Synagogue was established, there was a Jewish Cemetery here. To the north of this garden, in the eighteenth century, there was a home for the poor, which was demolished at the beginning of the nineteenth century. This area, which was enclosed by a wall until the outbreak of the Second World War, is connected with a legend, which explains the local tradition of forbidding marriage on Fridays. One Friday evening in Kazimierz there was a marriage that was running very late. The bride was an orphan. At the last minute the bridegroom refused to marry her because her dowry was smaller than that agreed in the pre-marriage conditions. Evening, and with it the Sabbath, had come before the missing sum could be collected. The wedding celebrations took place in a house opposite the synagogue and the old cemetery and went on late into the night with music and dancing. This flouting of the Sabbath caused great indignation in the Jewish town. The wedding guests, though, were impervious to appeals to stop the festivities, which prompted an infuriated Rabbi to excommunicate them. But a summary, and more severe, punishment was at hand: the ground was torn asunder beneath them and the wedding guests and the house they were celebrating in were swallowed up. After this the Rabbi forbade Friday marriages within the borders of the area administrated by the Jewish Council.

It is often the case that legends contain a grain of truth, and this one is no different. The wedding is an established fact. It took place in Kazimierz in the sixteenth century when Mojżesz Isserles-Remu was Chief Rabbi. But his part in the story was entirely different. It was the Rabbi himself who, wanting to help the orphan, brought the marriage about and, even though there was a real risk of violating the Sabbath, delayed the ceremony long enough for the full dowry sum to be collected and the conditions of the contract met. Then, when it was already one-and-a-half hours into the Sabbath, he gave the sign for prayers to begin. The whole affair produced two outcomes. First of all – and here again the legend is in accord with the truth – the council Elders did forbid Friday weddings. Second, there was a rabbinical dispute in which Rabbi Isserles was thunderously admonished. But he defended his decision steadily and logically saying that he had not departed from the principles of the Torah because the order not to perform marriages on the Sabbath did not come from that book but from the Rabbis. What is more, he argued, it is absolutely certain that the Rabbis made that law with no intention of causing the poor orphan distress.

The set of historical buildings and monuments made up by the New Synagogue and the adjacent Old Cemetery at Ul. Szeroka 40 is very much connected with Rabbi Mojżesz Isserles, who was also known as Rerau and is the most renowned of Polish Rabbis.

The New (Remu) Synagogue and the Old Cemetery

Enclosed by Ul. Szeroka, Miodowa, Jakuba, Ciemna and Lewkowa, this synagogue and cemetery occupy a small area of around one hectare.

Together they make up a unique complex of Jewish architecture and

The gates of the Remu Synagogue in the 1920s

art stretching back to the middle of the sixteenth century that continues to be the centre of Jewish religious life in Kraków. Sabbath and holiday services are conducted in the synagogue and the cemetery is visited by devout Jews from all over the world who come to pray by the graves of famous Kraków Rabbis, scholars and community Elders. As has been the case in the past, the largest number of pilgrims come to the Old Cemetery on the anniversary of Mojżesz Isserle's death (1525-72), which in the Jewish calendar falls on 18 Ijar (April/May).

The proximity of the cemetery and synagogue has few parallels as Judaism, in contrast to, for example, Christianity, maintains no sacral connection between the site of burial and the temple. We may conclude, then, that they were located so close together because of the extreme lack of space in the Jewish part of Kazimierz.

The Synagogue

This synagogue, which was, after the Old Synagogue, the second in the Jewish town of Kazimierz – and therefore originally named the New Synagogue – was built in 1553 at the eastern extreme of a parcel of land bought by the Jews and assigned to the cemetery. It was founded by Izrael ben Józef, the Chief Rabbi of the Jewish Community in Kraków, who was the nephew of Mojżesz Auerbach of Regensburg and the father of Mojżesz Isserles. It burned down in 1557 but was soon rebuilt thanks to permission granted Izrael ben Józef by King Sigismund II in the same year. The work was done by a Kraków architect, Stanisław Baranek.

The first women's prayer house was on the first floor of the wooden outhouse adjoining the synagogue's northern wall. Judging by its size, the synagogue was probably used by a small circle of the founder's family and friends.

It assumed its present architectural form in the process of a thorough restoration carried out in 1829. It was then that the western wall was rebuilt with the addition of the present women's prayer room next to it. This was connected by two rectangular arcades to the men's synagogue. The interior of the main room was given a new, wooden cradle vault to replace the old, stone one. The synagogue's semicircular eastern and western windows and the two-storey brick outhouse near the northern wall were the fruit of the same restoration. The next major restoration, carried out by the architect Herman Gutman, did not come until 1933. The work, which was mainly conservational, considerably improved the technical and aesthetic condition of the building without any significant change in its architectural appearance.

During the Nazi occupation of 1939–45 the synagogue was taken over by the German Trust Office (Treuhandstelle). The synagogue's main room was then used to store rubberised sacks for corpses, and the women's prayer room to store firefighting equipment – a purpose it continued to serve after 1945. The synagogue was stripped of its valuable ceremonial objects and the antique bimah and most of the furnishing was destroyed. After the war the Jewish Denominational Council again took over and, thanks to its efforts, the synagogue was restored in 1957. In the restoration some features of the interior decoration which, like the bimah, had been lost forever, were carefully recon-

The Remu Synagogue

structed. Where this could not be done new pieces were introduced.

After the Second World War significant changes were made on both sides of the gates leading to the synagogue's inner courtyard. In 1954 the single-storey house on the right hand side was demolished and this is why the brick wall there has an irregular shape. In 1994–5 a new restaurant was opened on the other side. Unfortunately, it does not at all suit the historical character of Ul. Szeroka. The old, brick gates leading to the synagogue's inner courtyard have been rather undermined and overwhelmed by the out-of-proportion metal framework of the restaurant's entrance a few metres to the left, with the whole effect serving only to demonstrate the investor's bad taste and conceit.

Only the top of the synagogue, with the semicircular window in the eastern wall and the low pyramidal shape of the hip roof, is visible from Ul. Szeroka. The remainder is obscured by the wall and gate. The gate features a tympanum decorated with a bas-relief, and has the Hebrew inscription, 'The New Synagogue: Dedicated to the Blessed Memory of Rabbi Remu'. But once through the gate and into the courtyard we are rewarded with a view of the strong, yet neither dense nor overbearing, line and body of this building and of the adjacent, lower, two-storey outhouse with vestibule and storage rooms. Set into the courtyard wall are tablets in memory of Kraków Jews who, in the main, were not part of the New Synagogue's congregation.

The Remu Synagogue is the Kraków Jews only active prayer house and therefore retains a special atmosphere in the unity of its formal and functional aspects that is absent from the remaining Kraków synagogues.

The vestibule is furnished with simple, contemporary objects: a table, benches and shelves for the prayer books and volumes of the Talmud. In the walls there are tablets recording when members of the congregation died. The prayer room entrance, which has a glazed wrought-iron door, is fringed with a sandstone portal, while in the door surround there is a stone alms-box in the shape of a renaissance portal. It carries a Hebrew inscription appealing to the congregation to give to the poor, 'gold, silver and brass' (Exodus 35:3), and to pray for Rabbi Mojżesz Isserles's soul. As in the vestibule, the prayer room floor is paved with nineteenth-century tiles. In the centre of this room, under the cradle vault, is a rectangular bimah, which lies on a low platform enclosed with wrought-iron work reconstructed to replace the one destroyed during the Second World War, and a lectern for the Torah. The bimah's polychrome double door, with bas-reliefs, dates from the eighteenth century and was brought here from another synagogue – very likely one outside Kraków. Its decorative elements are arranged symmetrically and show some affinity with folk art. On the door's outer side a vessel, from which an exuberant entanglement of branches with leaves, flower blossoms and fruit are emerging, is depicted. In the three, vertical ornamental areas on the inner side are a basket with fruit and flowers, two pitchers in bowls and a crowned menorah with flaming candles. The Holy Ark, from the late renaissance, is in the eastern wall. Its niche and Torah scrolls are en-

The bimah door in the Remu Synagogue

closed by an Art Nouveau, openwork door and veiled with a door curtain and lambrequin. The niche surround consists of a sandstone portal with double pilasters on both sides. Their capitals, which feature an untypical, ornamental pattern of vegetables, support the entire entablature and the frieze that has the Hebrew inscriptions, 'Look Down from Thy Holy Habitations, from Heaven, and Bless Thy People, Israel'

(Deuteronomy 26:15) and, 'By My Kings Reign' (Proverbs 8:15). In the copestone there is a rectangular plaque showing the Ten Commandments and a triangular pediment with bas-reliefs.

The composition of this surround bears a close resemblance to the Holy Ark in the nearby Old Synagogue. To the left of the ark, on the far pilaster, is a metal case for the eternal flame, or ner tamid, with the Hebrew inscription, 'An

57

Eternal Flame for the Soul of Remu, a Man of Blessed Memory'. To the right of the stairs leading to the platform, and in front of the ark, is the cantor's lectern. Before it is the shiviti board, which is indispensable to a synagogue. This consists of a simple frame with a portal drawn on it, and a text inscribed inside the drawing. The quotations are typical, 'I Have Set the Lord Always Before Me' (Psalms 16:8) and, 'Know Before Whom You Stand, Before the King of Kings Above all Kings, the Holiest One, May He Be Blessed' (The Talmud, Berachot treatise, 28b). Chandeliers, set on the pulpit and on the pedestal before the ark, are also an essential feature. To the right of the ark, above the row of chairs by the eastern wall, there is a partly reconstructed plaque commemorating where Rabbi Mojżesz Isserles used to pray, and one of the chairs is reserved in his honour. On the broader pilaster near to the southern wall is the foundation tablet, on which is written, 'Husband, Reb Izrael, son of Józef of

The Remu Synagogue and the Old Cemetery

blessed memory, bound in strength, to the glory of the Eternal One, and of his wife Małka, daughter of Eleazar, let her soul be received among the living, built this synagogue, the house of the Lord, from her bequest. Lord, restore the treasure of Israel'. The inscription's Hebrew text includes the date, 1553, when the synagogue was founded. To the right of the plaque are large marble tablets inscribed with the names of dead congregation members. Mounted

Prayers at the Old Cemetery on the anniversary of Rabbi Mojzesz Isserle's death (18 Ijar 1572), 1920s

within them are small light-bulbs that illuminate the panels during prayers for the dead.

The whitewashed walls of the prayer room are undecorated except for the twentieth-century murals on the western wall above the arcades that connect it to the women's section. They depict the wailing wall (the western wall: what remained after the demolition of the Jerusalem Temple),

Rachel's tomb and Noah's Ark. This intimate interior is completed with benches and desks arranged in several rows either side of the bimah and in single rows along the walls.

The Cemetery

Just behind the synagogue is the old cemetery. It is entered from the synagogue courtyard through a gate in the cemetery wall. The plaque above it states that it is, 'the Old Cemetery, burial place of Gaons, founded with the aid of the Kahal in the year (5) 311', that is, in 1552 of the Christian era. The plaque was transferred here in recent times from the original cemetery gate which, though bricked over, is still visible in the wall's central section in Ul. Jakuba.

There are very few Jewish tombs in Poland older than those in the Kraków cemetery. There are some from the twelfth and thirteenth centuries in Wroclaw, and some in Lublin, where the Jewish cemetery dates to 1540, making it just over a decade older than the Kraków necropolis. The Old Cemetery was closed in 1800, but some eminent people were still being buried there in the first half of the nineteenth century. Abraham Chaim, for example, the son of the well-known Warsaw and Kraków Rabbi, Ber Meisels, was laid to rest there in 1843. It was Rabbi Meisels who, in 1845, resisted a scheme to regulate town planning that may have meant encroachments on the cemetery. In a letter to the Senate of the Free City of Kraków he wrote that the graveyard, as the resting place of, 'leaders, lawgivers and teachers of the Jewish people' had immense religious and historical value. The Senate abandoned the project, perhaps taking the Rabbi's wise arguments into account. Thanks to this, the Old Cemetery occupies the same area now as it did then. It is unfortunate that the same cannot be said about the condition of the tombstones. From the end of the eighteenth century only minimal care was taken of the graveyard and this was mostly concentrated on the tombs of the eminent. In the interwar years its gener-

The Old Cemetery at the Remu Synagogue

al condition was poor. Here is a description from a contemporary guidebook, 'The monuments are, in the main, in a ruinous state and have either fallen to the ground, or are lying in piles before those that are still standing' (Bałaban, *Przewodnik*, p. 74).

During the Nazi occupation of 1939–45 the cemetery fell into utter ruin. The tombstones were broken, the wall was dismantled and it degenerated into an unofficial rubbish tip. After the Second World War only about a dozen tombstones remained in the cemetery. That one of these belonged to Rabbi Mojżesz Isserles was claimed by devout Jews as further proof of his saintly and miraculous power. It is said that the Nazis intended to destroy it but reconsidered when the first worker to touch it fell to the ground as if struck by a thunderbolt. In the middle of the 1940s, thanks to the Community's efforts, several dilapidated gravestones belonging to Kraków Rabbis were replaced with new ones. The cemetery was tidied up at the end of the 1950s and some archaeological excavations were conducted in its central area. Hundreds of tombstones, and many broken fragments of them, were found not far below the ground. More than seven hundred were put back

The Wailing Wall at the Old Cemetery

A Contemporary Kurhan at the Old Cemetery

uncovered during the restoration of the cemetery wall on Ul. Szeroka have been buried.

By far the majority of graves, though, are not in their original places and, because of this, and for reasons of conservation, the graveyard is more of a museum than a working cemetery.

in place on the surface. They were set on rectangular, stabilising concrete bases and arranged in straight lines, with both the rows and the tombs at regular distances apart. Many fragments were embedded in the inner side of the cemetery wall along Ul. Szeroka. In this way a unique wall mosaic of irregular chips of stone covered with Hebrew inscriptions, period ornaments and the motifs of Jewish sepulchral symbolism was created. After a while this became known as the 'Wailing Wall' because in representing the destroyed holy place of Kraków Jews it recalled the Wailing Wall in Jerusalem: likewise the remains of a destroyed temple and a holy place for all Jews. Nearby there is a stone burial mound topped with a slab. This is a relatively new tomb where bones

Since 1988 there have been a series of restorations aimed not at changing the gravestones in any way but at resisting their gradual destruction. The work has been paid for by the National Fund for the Restoration of Kraków's Monuments. Several stones have also been restored thanks to individual contributions.

The cemetery can be divided into three sectors:

Sector A – beginning near the entrance and comprising the first ten rows.

Sector B – the following nine rows extending along the western wall halfway along the cemetery and following Ul. Jakuba.

Sector C – the remaining rows with the tombs facing westwards in the opposite direction to those in sectors A.

The following people are buried in the Old Cemetery (Please note that the numbers denote row and grave):

Sector A
Beginning near the entrance and comprising the first ten rows.

A.1.6. Juda Lejb Landau, the son of Jekutiel Zelman, a merchant, who is referred to in the non-Jewish documents

The grave of Juda Lejb Landau

as Lewek. He died in 1632 and came from the influential Levite family the Landaus. His father, Jekutiel Zelman Landau, who died in 1614, was an Elder of the 'Council of the Four Lands', which was the representative body for the Polish and Lithuanian Jews. The grave is in the form of a sarcophagus. The frontal slab features a bas-relief of a pitcher, which is a symbol of the Levites.

A.6.1. Eliezer Damaszek, son of Józef, who was a rabbinical judge (dayyan) and the Chief Rabbi of Kraków in the first half of the nineteenth century. He wrote the responsa *Evnei Kodesh* (the Holy Stones). He died in 1847. On the tombstone one can see a stylised decoration featuring a nature scene with birds.

A.8.5. Izaak Landau, from the Levite family. He was Chief Kraków Rabbi from 1754–68 and died in 1768. The epitaph is flanked with fluted pilasters, while the tombstone is topped with three cones that have been arranged to replace lost statues of lions. Part of the epitaph reads, *'Our joy has turned to sorrow, the honour of Israel has been taken away and the crown has fallen from our head. Noble Rabbi, eminent Gaon, an example to our generation and our teacher and master'.*

▲ The grave of Izaak Landau

▼ The grave of Mordechaj Margulies

Sector B

The following nine rows extending along the western wall halfway along the cemetery and following Ul. Jakuba.

B.1.10. Mordechaj Margulies, Rector of Kraków's Rabbinical College from 1591-1617. He died in 1617. The pediment is decorated with an arch in the form of a stylized cartouche with small, vortical rosettes. Part of the epitaph reads, '*Here lies a man of God who shall be called a saint. He observed God's commandments and had great knowledge of law, casuistry, logic, the scriptures, the Mishnah and the Gemara*'.

B.1.13. Golda, daughter of the Lublin Rabbi Szalom Szachna. First wife of Rabbi Mojżesz Isserles (Remu). She died in 1552. A sarcophagus. The frontal vertical slab shows serious surface damage.

B.1.14. Gitel, daughter of Mojżesz Auerbach of Regensburg and grandmother of Rabbi Mojżesz Isserles (Remu). She died in 1552. Sarcophagus. In the nineteenth century its vertical frontal slab was re-cut and its original convex inscription was replaced by an engraved one. Part of the epitaph reads, 'All her life she was generous to the poor and she went to the synagogue every morning and night. Departed for eternal rest at a ripe old age (...) to join the world's righteous in the Garden of Eden'.

B.1.15. Miriam Bella, sister of Rabbi Mojżesz Isserles (Remu). She died in 1617. Sarcophagus. The frontal vertical slab we now see was made to replace the one destroyed in the seventeenth century.

B.1.16. Izrael ben Józef, merchant and banker. He founded the Remu synagogue and was the father of Rabbi Mojżesz Isserles (Remu). He died in 1568. Sarcophagus. The frontal vertical slab we now see was made to replace the one destroyed in the sixteenth century.

B.1.17. Mojżesz Isserles (c. 1525-1572), known as Remu, Chief Kraków Rabbi from 1547–72. He was President of the Rabbinical Court and Rector of the local Rabbinical College. He wrote many religious, philosophical and legal works, the most notable being *Darkei Moshe* (The Ways of Moses). This included his own commentaries on the ritual code by Józef Karo, *Szulchan Aruch* (The Prepared Table), which he adapted for the Ashkenazi Jews. These were very well-regarded and were later published

The Isserles family graves

together as *Mappa* (The Tablecloth). Sarcophagus. The frontal, vertical slab, which is from the eighteenth century, is decorated with exuberant tangles of grapevine and the Crown of Learning. The original slab, from the sixteenth century, has also been preserved and lies behind the frontal slab we see now. Part of the epitaph reads, 'Great scholar, light of the west, the greatest Gaon of his generation, our teacher, Rabbi Mojżesz, the Shepherd and Bastion of Israel. On the thirty-third day of Omer the honour of Israel was taken away. Moses was the shepherd of the flock of Israel, agent of God's law and His judgements over Israel, who spread knowledge among her people. From Moses unto Moses none among the equal'.

B.1.18. Izaak, known as Izaak the Rich, merchant and banker, brother of Rabbi Mojżesz Isserles (Remu). He was an Elder of the Jewish Community in Kraków. He died after 1585 but the exact date is unknown. Sarcophagus. The frontal slab was made after 1945.

B.1.19. Józef Kac, that is, Józef the priest, son of Mordechaj Gerszon, an eminent Talmudic scholar, author of the responsa (that is, works elaborating religious law in the form of questions and answers) *Szejrit Josef* (Jozef's Legacy) and valuable commentaries on the Talmudic writings of other authors. He was Rector of the Kraków Rabbinical College from 1576–91. He died in 1591. After his first wife died he married Józef Kac's sister and was therefore Mojżesz Isserle's brother-in-law. Because of this he lies among the Isserle family graves. The following names of those buried with him appear on the slab: his wife, Szprinca, his son Tanchum and his grandson, Gerszon, the son of Mojżesz. Sarcophagus. The frontal slab is a replica made after 1945.

B.1.29. Mojżesz Enzels, son of Naftale, the Chief Kraków Rabbbi from 1688–94. Mordechaj Deiches the son of Szymon Machlis and the Chief Kraków Rabbi in 1694-1706. The following people were buried with him: Jeruchem, son of Mordechaj Deiches, date of death unknown, Abraham, grandson of Mordechaj Deiches, date of death unknown, Kreindl, daughter of Abraham, died 1776. Sarcophagus with a wide frontal slab decorated with a carved crown that stands out sharply from the surface. The tomb was restored in 1924 thanks to the efforts of the Community.

B.1.32. Izaak Jakubowicz (reb Eisik, Jekeles). An Elder of the Kraków Community in the first half of the seventeenth century and a merchant and banker. In 1638–44 he founded the most

The grave of Isaak Jakubowicz

splendid of Kraków's synagogues, the Izaak, which was named after him. He died in 1653. Sarcophagus. Of the original only a part of the frontal slab with a cartouche remains. The rest is later. It is interesting to note that he has a second grave nearby. It was made after 1945, when it was thought that the original was irretrievably lost.

B.1.43. Natan Nata Spira (1583-1633), son of Salomon. He was President of the Kraków Rabbinical Court and Rector of the local Rabbinical College. Also a Kabbalist, he wrote *Megale Amukot* (Disclosures). Sarcophagus. Fragments of the seventeenth century frontal slab remain, while a replica slab, made after 1945, lies behind it. Part of the epitaph reads, 'Here lies a man of God, most saintly of ancestors, revealer of mysteries, secrets and treasures, he, whom they say spoke with the Prophet Elija face to face...' With him are buried Róża, died 1642, daughter of Mojżesz Jakubowicz and wife of Rabbi Natan Spira. Sarcophagus. Fragments of the seventeenth century frontal slab remain, while a replica slab, made after 1945, lies behind it. Dobrosz (Deborah), died 1642, daughter of Rabbi Natan Spira. Sarcophagus. Fragments of the seventeenth century frontal slab remain, while behind it is the replacement made after 1945 when the original was thought lost.

B.3.14. Drezel, daughter of Rabbi Mojżesz Isserles (Remu), wife of Symcha Bunem Meisels. She died before 1560. The tombstone is a late-nineteenth century replica.

B.3.15. Małka, mother of Rabbi Mojżesz Isserles (Remu). She died in 1552. The sepulchre is a late nineteenth century replica.

B.3.16. Mordechaj Saba, son of Jakub, known as Singe. A kabbalist and scholar of Hebrew grammar, he

The grave of Mordechaj Saba

followed Mojżesz Isserles as Rector of the Kraków Rabbinical School from 1572–76. He died in 1576. A bipartite sarcophagus with a coffer base and a high saddle-type retable. The vertical frontal slab with its concave inscription was remodelled in the nineteenth century. A part of the epitaph reads, *'This stone stands in memory of his spirit, which departed in peace. It is also witness to his eternal righteousness. From Mordechaj to Mordechaj none stood as this Mordechaj'*.

B.3.27. Eliezer Aszkenazi (1512–85), son of Elijah, Rabbi in Cairo, in Famagusta on Cyprus and in Poznań. Doctor and scholar. He wrote *Maasei Adonai* (The Works of the Lord). It would seem that he held no official post in Kraków. According to a legend he was miraculously, and instantaneously, swept from Cairo to Kraków on a Passover night during the Seder. He was able to finish his Passover meal in his new home in Poland.

▲ The grave of Eliezer Aszkenazi
▼ The grave of Joel Sirkes

Sector C

The remaining rows with the tombs facing westwards in the opposite direction to those in Sectors A and B.

C.1.4. Joel Sirkes (1561-1640), known as Bach. He was Chief Kraków Rabbi from 1618-40 as well as Rector of the local Rabbinical College. He was an eminent Talmudist and wrote many works including an extensive commentary to Jakub ben Aszer's (1296-1343) *Arba Turim* called *Bajt Chadasz* (The New House). His nickname comes from the first two letters of each word of the title. The tombstone is a replica that dates back to the eighteenth century and not the only one dedicated to Sirkes, because nearby there is a second made after 1945, when it seemed the original had been irretrievably lost.

C.1.21. Jozue ben Józef (1590-1648), Rector of the Kraków Rabbinical School and author of *Megina Szelomo* (Solomon's Shield). The tomb is a replica made at the end of the nineteenth century.

C.1.22. Jozue Heszel, son of Jakub, a Kraków Rabbi and Rector of the local Rabbinical College from 1654-63. The tombstone is a replica made after 1945.

C.1.26. Samuel bar Meszulam, he was doctor to two Polish kings: Zygmunt

Stary (the Elder) and Zygmunt August. He came to Kraków from Italy with the court of Princess Bona Sforza, who later married King Zygmunt Stary. He died in 1552. The undecorated sepulchral slab is made of reddish sandstone.

C.1.29. Izaak Lewita, son of Mordechaj. A Rabbi, he was President of the Rabbinical Court and Rector of the local Rabbinical College from 1776–99. He was son-in-law of the famous Arie Lejb, who was Rabbi in Rzeszów, Lemberg [Lwów] and Amsterdam. He was a staunch opponent of the Hassidic movement which he twice, in 1785 and 1797, excommunicated. The tombstone is of Dębnik black marble with bas-reliefs of a pitcher and basin, which indicate his membership of a Levite family. Ten graves further along the row the Rabbi has a second tomb, which is a replica made after 1945. Part of the epitaph reads *'The exquisite cypress withered when its branches fell. Who will shelter us, if there is no more heaven? Who will nourish our souls in a desert? Oh Lord! Oh Majesty! A just man, the pride of the world, the joy of a generation has perished. The earth radiated with his dignity'.*

C.1.74. Gerszon Saul Jomtow Lipman Heller (1579-1654), son of Natan. He was an accomplished scholar of the Talmud and the Mishnah and wrote

The grave of Izaak Lewita

many works on the subject. Particularly well-known is *fomtow's Supplement,* which concerns the six divisions of the Mishnah. He also wrote his autobiography, *Megilat ewa* (A Scroll of Hatred). Before coming to Kraków he was Rabbi in Vienna, Prague and in several small towns in eastern Poland. He became Chief Kraków Rabbi in 1643 and from 1648 he was also Rector of the local Rabbinical College. A sarcophagus with vertical slabs at front and back. The ornament engraved on the slab is a Levite

The grave of Lipman Heller

pitcher, which indicates that the dead man came from a Levite family. Thanks to the efforts of the Community this sepulchre has been restored many times.

It is here that we complete our visit to the Old Cemetery which, as the pantheon of Kraków Jewry, is worth every effort made to preserve it for future generations.

After returning to Ul. Szeroka from the Old Cemetery we go right and then, between the houses at numbers thirty-five and thirty-eight, we turn right into Ul. Lewkowa which runs along the cemetery wall behind the houses on Ul. Szeroka. On the left at Ul. Lewkowa

35, where there is now a police station, a floor beam has survived which bears the inscription, 'The Sceptre shall not depart from Judah' (Genesis 49:10). Concealed within the inscription is the date, 1667. From Ul. Lewkowa we turn right into Ul. Ciemna and can see the eastern wall of the Izaak Jakubowicz synagogue and the pre-Second World War Mizrachi prayer house that adjoins it on the synagogue's northern side. Via the short Ul. Izaaka we reach Ul. Kupa and are rewarded with a view of the synagogue's western facade at number sixteen.

The Izaak Jakubowicz Synagogue, circa 1925

The Izaak Jakubowicz Synagogue

The synagogue was founded by an Elder of the Kraków Kahal, Izaak Jakubowicz, who was granted permission to build by king Władysław IV on 30 April 1638. In 1639-40, however, no progress was made with the works because Marcin Kłoczyński, a priest and Prior of the monastic order of the Lateran Canons Regular, and Jakub Zadzik, Bishop of Kraków, protested against them. The building was finally completed and consecrated in 1644. It was then the biggest and most splendidly furnished of the Kazimierz synagogues. Its presence, among the pressed streets and smaller buildings close by, is monumental – an impression that must have been much stronger in the mid-seventeenth century, as the area where it was erected had just been incorporated into the Jewish town with its small, mainly wooden buildings. The walls were supported with buttresses – at the corners and on the longer elevation – and topped by a prominent cornice and a saddle roof. The shallowly-arched windows were arranged symmetrically with four in the southern and northern walls and two each in the eastern and western walls. There were also

The Izaak Jakubowicz Synagogue

single, semicircular windows in the eastern and western triangular gables. The entrance was placed asymmetrically in the southern wall and surrounded with an arcaded, rusticated portal of a type frequently seen in seventeenth-century Kraków architecture. There are external stairs, probably wooden when first built, leading to the women's gallery on the western facade.

The spacious interior has a cradle vault with lunettes richly decorated with stucco works similar to those visible on the vaults of St Mark's church and in the church of the Dominican Nuns in the Gródek district of Kraków.

The interior consists of the high men's prayer room, which measures 12 x 16.9m, and the women's gallery above the vestibule on the western side, which opens into the main hall with five arcades and Tuscan columns standing on the balustrade. The loggia is the most splendid in Kraków and has features in common with renaissance galleries. It was built by Jan Leitner, who was responsible for the cloisters in the Colleges of Medicine and Law and for those in the monastery of the Lateran Canons Regular in Kazimierz's Corpus Christi parish church.

The women's prayer room in the Izaak Jakubowicz Synagogue

One of the synagogue's interior architectural masterpieces was the bimah, which was modelled on that in the nearby Old Synagogue, but was unfortunately destroyed. The altar cupboard, with an ornamental gate and wrought iron work surrounding the platform and stairs in front of the ark, was also destroyed. During reconstruction work on the building in 1994-95 the ark was partly reconstructed. The work revealed fragments of murals completed from the seventeenth to the twentieth centuries. These were decoratively framed liturgical texts. Some of those from the seventeenth century have been identified and partly reconstructed.

In the nineteenth century, the main entrance was in the western facade. The exterior stairs leading to the women's room were once wooden and covered by a modest roof. The present two-way stairs with balustrades and a central arcaded porch were built by Zygmunt Prokesz in 1924. The left flight of these stairs led to the prayer room on the northern elevation, which was built by the same architect at the same time. In the north of the courtyard was a building for the synagogue staff with space to look after people who were profoundly deaf, which, again, was built in 1924. There was an extensive square in front of the synagogue which until 1939 was the site of a fish market. This was frequently photographed and has become an archetype of Kazimierz's past.

What exactly happened to the synagogue during the Second World War is not known. It was certainly not used for religious purposes and was probably stripped and ruined. In December 1939 an SS man murdered Maksymilian Redlich, an official of the Jewish Community, in the synagogue because he refused to carry out an order to burn it down.

After the Second World War, Jews who had come to Kraków from the Soviet Union lived in the synagogue.

In the 1950s it was taken over by the Artists' Union who adapted and restored it. By the middle of the 1970s the artists had left and the building became a sad, disused ruin. In 1983 the Kraków Historic Monuments Preservation Studio began renovation work to turn it into a specialized musical instrument workshop for the conservation of church organs. The former prayer house on the northern wall was reconstructed. Throughout the 1990s and until 2005 the Ronald R. Lauder Foundation's Centre for the Education of Jewish Youth was based in the building. Conservation work paid for by the National Fund for the

The fish market outside the Izaak Synagogue, 1907

Restoration of Historical Monuments in Kraków was carried out in 1994-5. This involved the synagogue's general restoration. During this work murals and the altar niche's stone surround were rediscovered and partially reconstructed. Reconstruction of the metal and stone bimah is also planned. The synagogue is now managed exclusively by the Jewish Community in Kraków. Since 1997 it has been open to citizens of Kraków and tourists alike who can enjoy the sight of its interior with its salvaged architectural details and polychrome wall decorations.

The Kupa Synagogue

Very close to the Isaak Synagogue, where Ul. Kupa and Ul. Jonatana Warschauera meet, is the last of the synagogues to have been built before 1650 and thus when the Jewish town existed. It was built thanks to Kahal funds (mikupat ha-kahal) and so is still known as Kupa. It was probably completed in the 1640s, an assumption supported by archival material stating that in 1643 the Guild of Jewish Goldsmiths donated four hundred Polish złoty for the work to be done. A fund was also raised by

The Kupa Synagogue

The eastern wall of the Holy Ark in the Kupa Synagogue

the Fraternity of Priests and Levites in 1647 for the southern window in the eastern wall near the ark, which is commemorated by a plaque that can still be seen in the synagogue.

The synagogue was put up near the northern section of the town's defensive wall between today's Ul. Jakuba and Plac Nowy on land set aside in 1609 for the development of the Jewish quarter, whose purchase was completed by 1635. In 1663 the synagogue was mentioned in a survey of part of the defensive wall destroyed during the war with Sweden. The survey tells us that there was a ritual slaughterhouse on the corner of Ul. Jakuba opposite the Jewish Cemetery to the east of the synagogue and, to the west of it, that there were wooden houses separating it from the Jordan family manor house in the Plac Nowy area. These may have had some connection with the Jewish Hospital, which was still there as late as the early years of the nineteenth century.

The synagogue's northern wall lay against the town defensive wall and was completely hidden by it. Originally, the synagogue was eighty centimetres lower than it is now and the men's prayer room was square. The women's section was in the northern part and was divided from the men's room by a wall with openings. The synagogue's most important interior elements, the bimah and the altar niche, were very similar to those in the other Kraków synagogues.

In the eighteenth century the town wall no longer had a defensive function. This meant that the synagogue's circumferential wall could be raised and more windows, admitting more light, could be built in the northern wall. It is also very likely that this was when the men's prayer room was covered with the wooden barrel vault described in 1829 during a survey for the roof's rafter framing. A small vestibule was added near the western wall and a women's gallery with a flight of wooden stairs leading to it from the outside was built over it.

In the 1830s it was thoroughly renovated. A two-storey annexe was built next to the western wall with a new vestibule on the ground floor and a women's gallery upstairs. Two further galleries, supported by wooden pillars, were added to the men's prayer room on its northern and southern walls. It was also given the flat, wooden ceiling that is still there today. The interior, meanwhile, was enlivened with new paintings and woodcarvings and the exterior elevations were made uniform.

In the second half of the nineteenth century the plot of land where the syna-

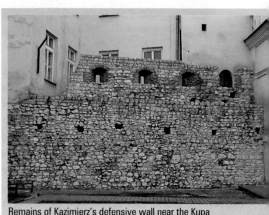

Remains of Kazimierz's defensive wall near the Kupa Synagogue

gogue stands, with a garden between the newly marked out Ul. Miodowa and the northern elevation, assumed its present form and extent. In the late nineteenth century the synagogue was enlarged with the incorporation of the brick building on its eastern side, which was thoroughly reconstructed and converted into additional prayer rooms: downstairs for the men and upstairs for the women.

Further modernization work, both in the synagogue itself and to make its surroundings more attractive, took place in the 1920s and 30s. A notable feature introduced at that time was the new decoration for the men's prayer room: illustrations of the Flood, a panorama of Jerusalem and the fate of the Jewish exiles in Babylon were painted on the western gallery's balustrade panels and the ceiling was painted and decorated in geometrical and symmetrical patterns featuring twelve medallions with biblical motifs The four corner medallions feature musical instruments from the Temple of Jerusalem, while in the remaining medallions – arranged in twos along each wall – there are views of cities, buildings and landmarks of Eretz Israel connected with history and biblical tradition: Hajfa, Hebron, Tybenada, the Gate of Jaffa, the Mamre Oak, the Wailing Wall, the Flood and the Sanctuary in Jerusalem. The synagogue's artistic decorations are not especially distinguished and we know nothing of who painted or designed them. During the interwar years various decorations with similar themes appeared in other Kraków synagogues including the New (Remu), the High, the Popper as well as in the prayer houses, such as the *Chewra Tehilim* at Ul. Meiselsa 18/Bożego Ciała 13. However only those in the Kupa synagogue and the *Chewra Tehilim* prayer house have survived and they are now the only remaining examples of this type of twentieth century Jewish art in Kraków.

During the 1939–45 German occupation the synagogue was severely damaged. The bimah – the platform before the ark – the stairs and the cantor's lectern were all completely destroyed. The moveable artistic furnishings were also completely lost.

For several years after the Second World War prayer services were again held in the synagogue and other, new functions were found for it. In 1946–7 matzohs were made there and in one of its rooms there was a ritual slaughterhouse for poultry, which operated until the death of the shochet, Abraham Lesman, in 1985. Some Jewish fami-

The Sunday market in Plac Nowy

lies who arrived from the Soviet Union after 1945 lived in the north-western outbuilding. After 1956 the Jewish Community leased it to the Saddler's Collective, which used it until 1991. During these years the synagogue deteriorated as it was being used neither appropriately, nor for its original purpose. In the 1990s it was again in the hands of the Jewish Community and in 2000–2001 it was thoroughly restored by the National Fund for the Restoration of Kraków's Monuments.

Plac Nowy

From the Kupa synagogue we move on in the direction of Plac Nowy.

On our way we pass a large building at Ul. Estery 6, on the corner with Ul. Warschauera.

Here, in the interwar years, was the Talmud Tora religious school, which was supported by the Community, and the Bejt Meir yeshiva: "A classroom: on the platform a young man with a long, brown beard in a round skull-cap is master of ceremonies. A book lies on a small stand in front of him. A strange kind of dialogue begins between him and one of the boys who sit around him on small benches. Rather than talking, though, they are singing a duet. Occasionally another boy, sitting next to the first one, butts in. The lad murmurs and then sings on. [...] Everyone is wearing long side curls and exquisite black yarmulkes, which gleam as if polished. The lesson comes to an end and they get up. They run past us and through the door. Some leave calmly: they have an austere composure and a dark, melancholy lustre in their eyes. Now another classroom: older boys bent over a fragment from the Talmud. The rooms are divided only by wooden screens and from all around come murmurs: the voices overlapping in this melodious learning. There are more than nine-hundred pupils in this massive old house. Such a school I have never seen before". (Alfred Döblin, *Podróż po Polsce, Journey through Poland*, p. 230).

Today's Plac Nowy was incorporated into the Jewish Town in the seventeenth century. Until 1822 there was a Jewish Hospital there which consisted of three wooden buildings for the sick and room for the staff. These buildings stood where the houses at numbers seven, eight and nine are today.

Plac Nowy is now widely known as Plac Żydowski. At its centre there is a circular market building from 1900, which is popularly known as 'the rotunda'. In 1927 it was leased by the Jewish Community as a ritual slaughterhouse for poultry. This was closed down by the Nazis when the occupation began and 'the rotunda' returned to its function as a market building.

Around Plac Nowy and in the streets leading into it are a number of friendly, cosy and imaginatively decorated pubs which, apart from offering something to drink, often have concerts and exhibitions.

Opposite 'the rotunda', on the first floor of the building at Ul. Estery 12, was Rabbi Chaim Halberstamm's Sądecki Hassidic prayer house. It is now a Christian charity called Brother Albert's House.

The single-storey corner building at Plac Nowy 5 and Ul. Meiselsa 17 is the old Bne Emuna prayer house. It was built in 1886 by Jacek Matusiński. It was used for a variety of business purposes after the Second World War and was once, for example, a carpenter's workshop. In 1988-93 it was renovated and adapted by Dariusz Gruszka to be the Judaica Foundation Jewish Cultural Centre. Most of the money came from the U.S. Congress with a much smaller amount coming from Kraków Council. The opening ceremony took place on 24 November 1993.

At the crossroads of Ul. Meiselsa, at number eighteen, and Ul. Bożego Ciała, at number thirteen, is the two-storey building with a characteristic arcaded frieze and semicircular, closed windows that was once the Psalm Fraternity (Chewra Thilim) prayer house. It was built in 1896 by Nachman Kopold. Inside are the very interesting remnants of wall paintings from the period 1918-39.

After leaving Plac Nowy and walking a short section of Ul. Estery we reach Ul. Miodowa. It was laid out in the nineteenth century more or less following the line of Kazimierz's old de-fensive wall. It was here that the Jewish Town ended and a new world distinguished by more modern architecture, but first of all by a different rhythm of life, began. Here, the influence of reformist tendencies in Jewish society, which gradually lost its uniformity over the nineteenth and twentieth centuries as a result of emancipation and secularisation, was prevalent. The immediate material symbols of this were several religious and educational institutions

Centre for Jewish Culture in the former Bne Emuna prayer house at Ul. Meiselsa 17

▲ The former Psalm Brotherhood prayer house on the corner of. Ul. Meiselsa and Ul. Bożego Ciała

▼ Ul. Rabbi Meiselsa 1930s: an Orthodox and Reform Jew on the way to their synagogues

founded in the second half of the nineteenth century and the first decades of the twentieth. These were the Tempel or Progressive Synagogue and elementary, middle and vocational schools founded from the general and religious Zionist movements. There was also a boarding school for Jewish students at university in Kraków.

The Progressive (Tempel) Synagogue

The first, makeshift prayer house for Reform Jews was established in Kraków in the early 1840s by mem-

The Progressive (Tempel) Synagogue in the 1930s

bers of the Religious and Civilizational Association under the leadership of Abraham Gumplowicz. According to its statute this 'German synagogue' (deutsche Schul) was to contribute to educating the young and expanding the intelligentsia. The association was to employ a preacher as a spiritual and moral guide and a teacher of religion who would be independent of the local Rabbi.

As the numbers of progressives grew the compact prayer room became inadequate. From 1858 therefore, the Board of the Synagogue started raising money to build a permanent temple. In November 1860 Ignacy Hercok's design for a new synagogue was approved

and the building was consecrated in 1862.

The synagogue stood on land beyond the historical borders of the Jewish Town in Kazimierz at the corner of Ul. Podbrzezie, which was demarcated before the synagogue was built, and Ul. Miodowa, which was built in the mid-1860s. The regularity of the elevations, the interior and choice of architectural decoration were, in general terms, a reference to the 'Temple' style of synagogue then being built in German towns and in Vienna, which was similar then in many respects to Kraków. In 1892–94 the synagogue was extensively reconstructed to take the form we now see. The work was done by the architect Beniamin Torbe, and mainly involved extending the building on its eastern side and remodelling the western facade. The walls were raised slightly. The lateral elevations were extended eastward but their former character was retained with the continued use of bipartite windows on each floor. The prayer room was enclosed on its eastern side with a pentagonal apse, while the synagogue's south and north-eastern corners were symmetrically covered with arcaded porches that concealed the landings and the stairs to the women's galleries. The western facade was raised by adding an extra section to the pediment. In 1898 a new ark was installed which, in its ideological and formal aspects, showed some affinities with Christian sacral architecture. It was made from Carrara marble by the Kraków sculptor, Fabian Hochstim, and was funded by the President of the Kraków Jewish Community, Leon Horowitz. The interior decoration includes murals and stucco work as well as stained-glass windows signed and dated by their founders, which were introduced from 1894.

The building as it stands today assumed its final form in 1924 when the aisles, which are shorter than the main building, were added on the first-floor. The bipartite windows in them copied the form and pattern of the ear-

The Progressive Synagogue in Podbrzezie, circa 1905

lier windows and this maintained the building's overall style. Contemporary stained-glass panels were added to the aisle windows. The reconstruction work carried out at the end of the nineteenth century and in the interwar years was augmented by efforts to improve the site. As early as 1894 the building was screened with a pilaster fence on the Ul. Miodowa side.

Services in the Progressive Synagogue were conducted according to principles developed by German Rabbis in the 1840s at conferences in Brunswick, Frankfurt and Wrocław. In formal terms they were closer to Christian services than those in traditional synagogues. A weekly sermon given alternately in Polish and German by a preacher with an academic background was introduced to the Progressive synagogue. The most eminent of these was Dr Ozjasz Thon, who preached sermons here from 1897 until his death in 1936. The liturgy was accompanied by choral singing to organ music. In the interwar years women sang in the choir.

During the German occupation of 1939–45 the Tempel was converted into a storage room and the aisles served as a stable for horses. Religious services returned soon after the end of the

▲ The facade of the Progressive Synagogue

▼ The ark in the Progressive Synagogue

A stained-glass window in the Progressive Synagogue

war. Because not only Progressives but traditional Jews as well prayed in the Tempel the present bimah was introduced. At the same time a prayer room for Orthodox Jews was established in one of the outbuildings. In 1947 a ritual bath was opened in the northern group of outbuildings.

It was only occasionally that services were held in the synagogue af-

ter 1968 and by 1981 they had almost completely ceased. From 1995, after a period of disuse and disregard, a thorough renovation began with the support of the World Monuments Fund and the National Fund for the Restoration of Kraków's Monuments. The Tempel has become the traditional venue for the opening concert of the annual Festival of Jewish Culture.

A concert given by the Cantor's Choir in the Progressive Synagogue

From the synagogue we take further steps along Ul. Podbrzezie until we reach number six which, in the interwar years, was the site of the Crafts (Boarding) School for Jewish orphans. There is a plaque on the building commemorating philanthropist, school president and Kraków city councillor Sinaj (Zygmunt) Aleksandrowicz (1877-1946).

The next part of our stroll along Ul. Podbrzezie takes us to a corner building on our left at the crossroads with Ul. Brzozowa, which features two memorial plaques – in Hebrew and Polish – containing information about its former function. There was a Primary School at Ul. Brzozowa 5, while at Ul. Podbrzezie 8-10 there was the Chaim Hilfstein Hebrew Secondary School.

Finally, at Ul. Podbrzezie 3, there was the Secondary Arts and Craft School of the Jewish Association of Folk and Secondary Schools in Kraków. From 1934 the secondary school enjoyed full public rights meaning that pupils with its leaving certificate were entitled to attend Polish universities. This significantly increased its attractiveness. The school, which focused on the humanities, operated in two languages: general subjects were taught in Polish and Judaic subjects in Hebrew. Learning revolved around Poland and its culture so that even subjects to some degree remote from this theme were nevertheless made relevant to it. In this way German and Latin were employed to describe Kraków, narrate Polish legends and tales and to discuss contemporary events. The other pathway in the teaching and upbringing the school provided was that of Jewish culture. High educational standards were ensured by the excellent teaching staff, which included the school's Director Hirsz Szerer, who was a mathematician, the poet, philologist of Polish and translator of French and German literature, Juliusz Feldhon, the writer and philologist of Polish, Chaim Löw, the naturalist and Jagiellonian University lecturer, Joachim Metallmann and the Jagiellonian University Hebrew scholar and teacher of Hebrew, Bencjon Katz. Meanwhile, the school prayer house, *Nachlat Awot*, set up on the initiative of young people in 1931, played a major role in the cultivation of the Jewish tradition beyond the compulsory educational programme. It was the scene of daily morning prayer, Saturday and holy day services as well as other special religious gatherings – especially confirmation (*bar micwa*) for the boys at the school when they reached the age of thirteen.

We need only walk a few metres from here to the house at Ul. Brzozowa 6 where we can see, at the back, the former Solomon Deiches prayer house, which was built in 1910 by Henryk Lamensdorf. It is a two-storey building with a terrace upstairs and stone tablets with the Ten Commandments at the top of the facade.

From Ul. Brzozowa we cross into the nearby Ul. Berka Joselewicza, where the house at number five has a plaque commemorating Mordechaj Gebirtig, a famous folk poet and the bard of the Jewish street. He was born in Kraków on 4 May 1877 and was murdered on 4 June 1942 during a mass expulsion from the ghetto to the death camps. He came from a poor

Gilbert Levine conducting the Kraków Philharmonic at the Progressive Synagogue

family and remained among the poor all his life. His education went as far as the cheder, which taught Hebrew and religious knowledge, and he earned his living as a carpenter and, later, as a furniture restorer in his brother Leon's workshop at Ul. Starowiślna 28. Around 1909 he married Bluma Lindenbaum. They had three daughters: Charlotte, Ewa and Leonora. Of great sensibility and talent, he performed at the Jewish amateur theatre and wrote poems and songs that were sung on the Jewish street – though few when they heard them could recall the writer's name. He composed the melodies himself but it is likely that he did not know how to write them down and turned to musicians he was friendly with and, particularly, to the composer and musicologist Juliusz Hoffmann. His most well-known songs include *Kinderjorn* (Childhood Years), *Rejzele (Rejzele), Unzere sztetl brent* (Our Village is Burning) and *Blajb gezunt mir* (Say Farewell to Kraków). Many of the verses he wrote in Yiddish have been translated by Natan Gross, Jerzy Ficowski and Agnieszka Osiecka. In Poland Gebirtig's songs are performed

▲ The commemorative plaque on the wall of the Hebrew Secondary School on the corner of Ul. Podbrzezie and Ul. Brzozowa
▼ Facade of the Salomon Deiches prayer house at Ul. Brzozowa 6

by Golda Tercer and Sława Przybylska among others. (Gross, *Żydowski Bard*).

We now visit another outstanding Krakowian, Dr Ozjasz Thon (1870-1936). He lived at Ul. Bogusławskiego 5 – once Ul. Jasna – on the other side of Ul. Dietla, the street that separates Kazimierz from Stradom. He was Rabbi and Preacher at the Tempel (Progressive) Synagogue as well as being a politician and journalist. In the interwar years he was leader of the Zionist Movement and President of the Kraków Jews. His residence here is justly commemorated by a plaque.

Returning to Kazimierz we follow Ul. Starowiślna as far as the crossroads with Ul. Miodowa, turn left, walk under the railway bridge, and reach the gates of the New Cemetery at Ul. Miodowa 55.

The New Cemetery

The so-called New Jewish Cemetery lies in an area of about 4.25 hectares between the embankment of the Kraków-Tarnów railway line, Ul. Miodowa, Ul. Siedleckiego and Ulica Daszyńskiego. It is separated from Ul. Miodowa by the cemetery wall, by a brick, pre-burial hall and by a two-storey residential building on the hall's eastern side. It was established in 1800 on land beyond the built-up area of Kazimierz bought by the Community from the Augustinian monks. It was extended in 1836 after the purchase of a piece of adjacent land – again from the Augustinian monks. It was extended several times in the interwar years but was still not big enough. Therefore, in 1926, the Community bought land in Wola Duchacka – a village near Kraków – for another cemetery. It was consecrated on 6 April 1932.

Memorial to Nazi victims in the New Cemetery on Ul. Miodowa

Although it was closed during the Nazi occupation, the caretaker, Pinkas Lander, and his family lived at the New Cemetery from 1941–43 when the Podgórze ghetto existed. After this ghetto was liquidated he was taken to the Płaszów camp and executed in Autumn 1943, 'The caretaker was probably killed to get rid of a witness to the German's business dealings in selling the most precious gravestones to various stone-cutters. Some were taken to the Płaszów camp – then being built – and laid as a pavement leading to the camp office. An engineer, Stendig, found some of these in the area of the former camp, including one belonging to Dr Ozjasz Thon, then a Rabbi and, before the war, a member of the Polish Parliament. These were re-turned to the New Cemetery. In August 1944, under the escort of some SS men, Stendig was taken to the cemetery in Ul. Miodowa and asked to select some grave-stones for the camp. He then discovered that a twenty-metre wide area had been demarcated parallel to the railings along the whole length of the cemetery to build a school for railway workers. The tomb-stones in it were pulled down, the graves were opened and the bones, as well as some ceremonial objects, were scattered about the dug ground'. (Bieberstein, *Zagłada*, p. 230).

The pre-burial hall at the New Cemetery on Ul. Miodowa

After 1957 it was tidied up with the assistance of the Joint Distribution Committee, an American organization channeling the efforts of a variety of institutions established to aid the Jews, and remains to this day a functioning Jewish cemetery.

Anyone who has even once visited this cemetery will have found it striking that, apart from the older, original tombstones there are many new ones. Their inscriptions are dedicated to Jews killed in the death camps and throughout Poland during the Nazi occupation, and to Jews killed in other European countries. Pieces of old, broken sepul-

chral stones have been embedded in the cemetery wall and in the foundations of the tombstones on the Ul. Miodowa side. These 'mosaics' are a particular feature of the Jewish cemeteries preserved in Poland and are found in almost all of them. Behind the wall separating the cemetery from the street, to the right of the gate, there is a large, somewhat shabby, rectangular monument. On it rests a block of black marble bearing the image of a seven-stemmed candelabrum symbolizing Judaism and Jewishness. It is dedicated to, 'the memory of murdered Jews, victims of the Nazi genocide 1939-45'. The plaques commemorate

ly juxtaposed language with their partly preserved Hebrew inscriptions and the symbolic ornaments hewn in the stone.

A wide alley cuts through the cemetery from the axis of the pre-burial hall, with two narrower alleys running perpendicular to the main alley. But the old cemetery layout has been considerably altered by graves constructed after the war. These were often put in the passages between the rows as this was the only space available. The most recent graves are on the south-western side near the wall that runs along the railway embankment. They are no different from the graves in Polish Catholic cemeteries and resemble them not only in the shape of the gravestones but also with respect to the flowers, wreaths and cemetery candles that are brought to the cemetery at the time of burial and placed on the graves by loved ones on the anniversaries of those deceased.

The oldest graves, in the traditional matzevah form with semicircular tops and Hebrew inscriptions, date back to the 1840s. Typical Jewish sepulchral symbols are visible on their pediments. Gradually, over the second half of the nineteenth century and the twentieth century, tombstones ceased to be built with the characteristic symbolic matzevah features. Rather, they fol-

The interior of the pre-burial hall

individual Jews, as well as whole families, who perished in those years – often in unexplained circumstances. One is dedicated to Dr Rafał Landau and his wife Rachel Parnes. Both died in the Soviet Union in 1941. Landau, a barrister, was the last President of the Jewish Community in Kraków before the war. There are also pieces of nineteenth century tombstones embedded in the walls of the monument, which render an odd-

The grave of Maciej and Czesław Jakubowicz

lowed contemporary trends in public art and were frequently little different from those in Christian cemeteries. The presence of epitaphs in Polish and German was another new phenomenon and reflected trends toward secularisation and cultural assimilation among the Kraków Jews.

Majer Bałaban, describing the New Cemetery in the interwar years, mentions around fifty eminent people buried there. They are Rabbis from Kraków and elsewhere, dayyans, Hassidic theo-

reticians, Haskalah scholars, Hebraists, doctors, politicians and artists (Bałaban, *Przewodnik*, pp. 103–6). Unfortunately, the majority of the monuments dedicated to them were destroyed during the Nazi occupation.

We now proceed along the cemetery's main alleyway from the pre-burial hall. Among those buried there are:

Jakub Drobner (1827-96), a doctor who took part in the January rising of 1863-4 against the Russian partition.

Jerzy Gert (1908-68), conductor and composer, organiser and artistic director of the Polish Radio Orchestra and Choir in Kraków, with which he made more than four thousand recordings – mostly of Polish classical and popular music.

Maciej Jakubowicz (1911-79) and **Czesław Jakubowicz** (1925-97), who were both presidents of the Jewish Community in Kraków during the very testing period following the Second World War.

Samuel Stendig (1900-42), philologist, teacher at the Hebrew Secondary School and director of the specialist Business Secondary School. He was also a journalist and author and wrote numerous papers and articles on educational matters, as well as pamphlets in support of Zionism. The engineer Jakub Stendig erected a symbolic memorial to him in the graveyard after the war.

Ozjasz Thon (1870-1936), Rabbi, politician, journalist and deputy in the Parliament of the Second Republic. He came from Lwów and studied Philosophy and Sociology at the University of Berlin and at that city's Rabbinical Academy. While studying he began to work with Teodor Herzl, the father of modern political Zionism. In 1897 he accepted the invitation of Kraków's Reform, or Progressive, Jews to take on the role of preacher in their synagogue. In 1919 he was a Jewish delegate at the peace conference in Versaille. He was leader of the Western Małopolska and Śląsk Zionist Organisation in 1919-36, co-founder and president of the *Tarbut* (Culture) schools and co-founder of the Institute for Judaic Studies in Warsaw. He also wrote essays and articles both for the press and for an academic audience and published in Hebrew, Yiddish, German, Polish and English in Jewish newspapers and journals – especially in the Kraków, Polish language *Nowy Dziennik* (New Daily).

On reaching the grave of Ozjasz Thon we turn right. In the sections along this alley the following Jews are buried or commemorated with symbolic memorials:

Mordechaj Gebirtig (Marcus Bertig, 1877-1942), poet, singer and actor. He wrote the folk songs, lullabies and stage duets that were the hits of Jewish theatre revues. He published a slim volume of verse *Folkstimlech* (*Na ludową nutę,* Of the Folk, *1*920) and the collection *Majne Lider (Moje pieśni,*

▲ The grave of Jerzy Gert

▼ The grave of Ojzasz Thon

My Songs, 1936). His late poetry, written during the Second World War, was collected in *S'brent* (*Gore!*, It's burning, 1938). He was killed during ghetto clearances on 4 July 1942. His most famous song, *S'brent*, became the anthem of the fighting youth of the ghetto. It is traditionally sung at ceremonies held in memory of those who were killed in the holocaust.

Jan Landau (1871-1936), a socially engaged paediatrician, co-founder and long-term president of the Association for the Care of Jewish Orphans in Kraków and co-founder and president of the Kraków branch of the Jewish People's Healthcare Association. In 1924-36 he was director of the Jewish hospital in Kraków and the driving force behind its modernisation and expansion. He was active in the work of care and aid groups, whose aim was to broaden access to education and raise standards of healthcare.

In the sections of the cemetery that lie along the railway embankment, where there are now also new graves, the following are buried:

Zofia Ameisenowa (1897-1968) was an art historian and outstanding humanist with a profound knowledge

97

of miniature European painting. She was the author of very highly regarded works on iconography, religious symbolism and the history of art.

Wilhelm Berkelhammer (1889-1934), journalist and lawyer. From 1918 until his death he was editor-in-chief of the Kraków newspaper *Nowy Dziennik* (New Daily), which was the first Jewish newspaper in Europe to be published in the language of the country of settlement and was the organ of the Western Małopolska and Śląsk Zionist Organisation.

The Frankels were a family of industrialists and philanthropists. Wilhelm (1844-1920) was co-director of the Portland Cement factory in Bonarka and a generous donor to the Rabka Sanatorium for Jewish Children. Maria (1852-1931), born Liban, was Wilhelm's wife and co-owner of the Portland Cement factory in Bonarka. She also sponsored the Rabka Sanatorium for Jewish children, which was later named after her. Henryk (1871-1937), son of Maria and Wilhelm, was an industrialist and director of the Bernard Liban and Co. cement factory in Bonarka. He co-founded both the Austrian cement cartel and the Faience and Fireclay Products Factory in Skawina. His civic activity included being a Podgórze town councillor and funding the building in Kraków of the vocational secondary school for Jewish girls known as *Ognisko Pracy*. Its director for many years was Henryk's wife, Eliza (1882-1957), born Berggrün, who was a teacher and educationalist.

Adolf Gross (1862-1936), a politically and socially engaged lawyer and town councillor. He was a co-founder of the League of Independent Jews, which worked for the real equality of the Jewish people, and was editor of its mouthpiece *Tygodnika* (The Weekly). In 1907 he established one of the first housing associations in Poland and, as a town councillor, directed the Association for the Building of Cheap Houses in Kazimierz.

Artur Markowicz (1872-1934). A painter, he studied at the Kraków School of Fine Arts, the Academy of Fine Arts in Munich and at the School of Fine Arts in Paris. He belonged to the *Sztuka* association of Polish artists as well as to the Jewish Association of Artists, Painters and Sculptors in Kraków. When young he painted landscapes but, with time, scenes from the life of traditional Jewish society began to dominate. In this way he acquired the nickname 'the ghetto painter'. He was an astute and painstaking observer and a superb draughtsman. His painting is characterised by realism and the capture of a range of moods.

Józef Sare (1850-1929), architect and builder responsible for many of Kraków's public buildings. He was the first Jew to hold the office of vice-president of the city (1905-29) and he oversaw the city's finances as well as the critical and sensitive communal undertakings of water, gas and transport.

One of the most recent graves in this section of the cemetery is that of **Henryk Halkowski** (1951-2009) who was a philosopher, journalist and translator and also a great advocate for the establishment of an institute in Kraków dedicated to researching the spiritual culture of Ashkenazi Jews.

Immediately next to the cemetery wall that runs along the railway embankment are the sections containing the graves of soldiers. They date from the First World War and follow the principle observed in the Austrian army of burying soldiers either in new, denominational cemeteries or in the sections allotted for war graves in existing denominational cemeteries. In 1936-7 work was undertaken to restore these graves with the financial resources needed coming from collections made by the Jewish Union for Polish Independence and from the local denominational council budget. A total of 324 Jews were laid to rest there – initially in 161 individual and 14 collective graves. These were soldiers who fought

The grave of Józef Sare

in the risings of 1848 and 1863, *Sybiracy* (Siberians) and the fallen from battles for Polish Freedom in 1914-21 who had won Military Crosses, Poland's highest military decoration for courage, Crosses of Independence and Crosses of Valour. All of the gravestones were made according to the same design. The inscriptions included name, surname and rank and, in some cases, honours awarded. The sections containing the graves were divided from each other by slab paths, while a sturdy metal fence enclosed the whole of this part of the cemetery. The war graves were destroyed on orders from the Germans during the Second World War. Only a few of the original memorials now remain.

The following, amongst others, are laid to rest in the war graves adjacent to the wall on the Ul. Daszyńskiego side:

Ignacy Ehrenpreis (1873-1937), industrialist. He ran the family business *Liban i Ehrenpreis*, a lime quarry and works, as well as a ceramics factory. As an advocate of assimilation he was vice-president of the Association of Progressive Jews which maintained the Progressive Synagogue in Kraków. For many years he served on the town and Jewish Community councils.

The Epsteins, a family of industrialists active in local business life. **Juliusz** (d. 1914), a banker and industrialist, established and owned the iron works and iron and steel-rolling mill at Borek Fałęcki, as well as a wire and nail factory in Podgórze. He was a Podgórze town councillor and for forty years a member of the Kraków Chamber of Commerce. His son **Tadeusz** (1870-1939), also an industrialist, was engaged in social and business affairs. In 1903 he was chosen as a town councillor and was successfully involved in the public and business life of Kraków. He was leader of the Chamber of Commerce for many years and organized money and cereal markets in Kraków. He was active in several economic and financial organisations and took charge of his father's businesses. His deep commitment to society at large meant that self-enrichment was not his priority and he therefore died in poverty.

Maurycy Gottlieb (1856-79) A painter, he studied at the academies of fine art in Vienna, Munich and Kraków. His work reveals a romantic nature, creative turmoil and an inner conflict arising from a drive to identify and interpret his own national identity. He painted historical, literary and biblical

The grave of Maurycy Gottlieb

Castle. He also worked with other Kraków stonemasons on the restoration of the *Sukiennice* in 1875-79. In 1898 he produced a monumental altar cabinet of Carrara marble for the Progressive Synagogue in Kraków. He is the author of several grave memorials in the New Jewish cemetery on Ul. Miodowa, including a memorial obelisk (1892) for the painter Maurycy Gottlieb.

Nachman Kopald (1834-1911), architect and builder. In 1870-90 his work mainly involved designing and building private apartment buildings in Kraków. He was also responsible (1896) for the *Chewra Tehilim* (Psalm Brotherhood) prayer house at the intersection of Ul. Meiselsa and Ul. Bożego Ciała in Kazimierz.

Ignacy Krieger (1817-89) A photographer, he produced thousands of documentary photographs of artistic and architectural monuments, views of the city and its surroundings as well as portraits of its inhabitants, including Kraków's Jews. These are all now very highly regarded.

Leon Sternbach (1884-1940) A classical philologist and manuscript expert, he was one of the world's

themes. However it was his portraits that brought him fame and recognition. His oeuvre is firmly grounded in the Jewish religious tradition and in the culture of Polish romanticism. He is regarded as the greatest Polish artist of Jewish descent.

Fabian Hochstim (1825-1906) A stonemason and sculptor, he worked alongside Jan Matejki on the restoration of the gothic marble sarcophagus of King Kazimierz the Great at Wawel

greatest Byzantine specialists. He published groundbreaking research and criticism on Greek and Byzantine texts and also studied Saint Gregory of Nazianzus. Sternbach was a member of the Academy of Arts and Sciences in Kraków and of numerous international associations. He was arrested on 6 November 1939 together with other Jagiellonian University professors and was taken to the Sachsenhausen concentration camp and executed.

Jonatan Warschauer (1820-88), socially engaged doctor. His major research interests were epidemiology and balneology. He was a member of the Academy of Arts and Sciences and President of the Kraków Medical Association. As a town councillor from 1848 he made great efforts to establish the city's water supply system. He played a leading role amongst the intelligentsia of the Progressive Kraków Jews and was one of the prime movers of the pro-Polish *Przymierza Braci* (Covenant of Brothers) which advocated the assimilation of Jews into Polish culture. In his will he left his wealth to be used for the assistance of the needy of all religious persuasions. The old Ul. Ubogich in Kazimierz is now named after him.

The grave of Jonatan Warschauer

Kraków Orthodox and Hassidic Rabbis lying at rest in the new cemetery:

Szymon Schreiber (1820-83) Rabbi, member of the Austrian parliament and the foremost Orthodox leader in Galicia. He came from a rabbinical family in Frankfurt. He was a Rabbi first in Mattersdorf and then from 1860 in Kraków. The years of his Rabbinate coincided with a period of acute struggle between traditionalists and those who favoured change. Opposed to assimilation, he rose to be the outstanding leader of Orthodoxy in Galicia and was instrumental in bringing about a covenant between Orthodoxy and the Hassidic movement. In 1879, together with the zaddik, Joshua Rokeach, he established the *Machzike Ha-Dat* community (Upholders of the Religion). A collection of his sermons, *Miktaw Sofer*, was published in Jerusalem in 1952.

Akiba Kornitzer (1838-83), Rabbi. He was the grandson of Moses Schreiber *(chatam sofer)* the great Rabbi of Pressburg (Bratislava). Thanks to his marriage to the daughter of the Rabbi of Kraków (Szymon Schreiber) he found himself, after Schreiber's death, in the thick of the struggle for power in the community. As an Orthodox Rabbi close to the Hassidics he found the Progressive intelligentsia and the council of the Jewish Community in Kraków ranged against him. He was judge in the rabbinical court and also leader of the extreme orthodox community in Kraków. He was the father of Józef Nechemiasz Kornitzer, the final Kraków Rabbi before the Second World War.

Józef Nechemiasz Kornitzer (1880-1933), Rabbi. He graduated from the Talmudic Academy in Pressburg (Bratislava) and became Rabbi in Wielki Sewlusz, now Wynohradiw in Ukraine. In 1924 The Jewish community in Kraków chose him as Rabbi. He was a great authority on religious matters. Apolitical, he resisted pressure both from the Orthodox trying to take power in the Community and from Zionists expecting support on the Palestinian question. He was the final Rabbi of Kraków before the outbreak of the Second World War.

Samuel Szmelkes Kornitzer (1905-41), Rabbi and son of Józef Nechemiasz Kornitzer. From 1933 he was judge in the Rabbinical Court and from 1935 he was Rabbi of the Jewish Community in Kraków. In 1940 he attempted to resist the expulsion of Jews from Kraków by asking Prince Adam Sapieha, Metropolitan Archbishop of Kraków, to intercede in his capacity as president of the Central Welfare Council. In retaliation for seeking this intervention the Germans, in February 1941, threw him into KL Auschwitz where he was executed.

Kalman Kalonimos Epstein (1754-1823), Hassidic leader who was known as the holy *Maor Vashemesh* after the title of his work *Maor wa-Szemesz*. He was taught by outstanding zaddiks, such as Elimelech of Leżajsk and Jakub Izaak ha-Choze (the seer) of Lublin. As early as 1875 he had organised the first group of Hassidics in Kraków and this met with considerable resistance from the official Jewish Community. He was twice excommunicated by the presiding Rabbi and his Rabbinical Court. His major work, *Maor wa-Szemesz* (From the Light and the Sun), is one of the integral texts of Hassidic literature and was published by his son in 1842 after Kalman's death. It is written in the form of a commentary on the Torah and includes a description of the life and works of many of the Hassidic leaders of that epoch.

Aron Epstein (d.1882), Kalman's son, was leader of the Hassidics in

The graves of Kalman and Aron Epstein

Kraków. He carried on the work begun by his father, for example in publishing his father's work, *Maor wa Szemesz* (From the Light and the Sun), and in spreading Hassidism in Kraków and western Galicia. He established the first Hassidic prayer house in Kraków: *Reb Arons Klaus* at Ul. Józefa 33 in Kraków.

The New Cemetery is the last stage but one in the tour of Kraków's Jewish historical buildings and monuments. For the final stage we leave the cemetery and, taking the shortest route by following Ul. Halicka along the line of the railway embankment, reach Ul. Przemyska. There, at number three, was the former Jewish Student Hall of Residence, which was built in 1924–26 by the Kraków branch of the Bnei brit (Solidarity) Association and the 'Ognisko' Association of Jewish Jagiellonian University Students. The money came from the University and donations from Kraków Jews. The design was prepared by Adolf Siódmak, while the interior decoration was the work of another architect, Tobiasz Wexner, who was also in charge of the building works. The five-storey building had rooms with showers and washbasins for one-hundred-and-forty students sharing in twos and threes. There was also a library, a student refectory and kitchen, an art studio on the top floor and, on the second floor, a large meeting room.

The hall became an important centre of Jewish social and cultural life. In the 1930s, for example, members of the Association of Jewish Artists, Painters and Sculptors often showed their work in the meeting room. The artists included Artur Markowicz, Abraham Neumann, Szymon Müller, Wilhelm Grünberg, Leon Lewkowicz, Antoni Soldinger, Jakub Glasner and Henryk Hochmann. In October 1939, after it had been abandoned by students, the Germans opened a brothel for the army there. They made similar use of an old people's home for Jews in Ul. Skawińska Boczna, which had just been completed when the occupation began. Now, as before, the building is a student hall of residence and is used by students of Kraków's College of Music.

We conclude our journey around the Jewish historical buildings and monuments of Kraków on Ul. Przemyska and now turn to the extermination of the Kraków Jews in the Second World War. We leave Kazimierz, and follow Ul. Starowiślna over the Wisła to reach the Podgórze district. It was here that the most important stages of the extermination took place, and it is here that we find the places of remembrance.

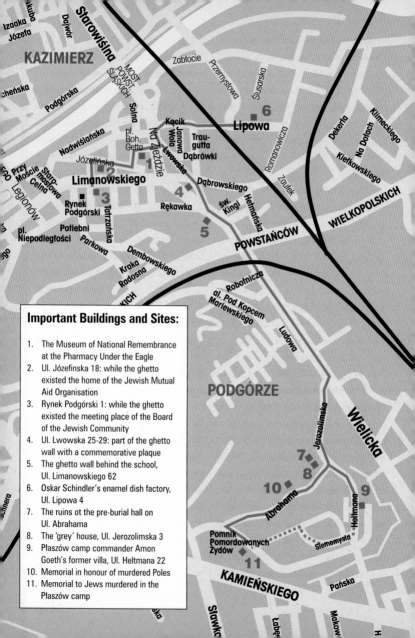

Important Buildings and Sites:

1. The Museum of National Remembrance at the Pharmacy Under the Eagle
2. Ul. Józefinska 18: while the ghetto existed the home of the Jewish Mutual Aid Organisation
3. Rynek Podgórski 1: while the ghetto existed the meeting place of the Board of the Jewish Community
4. Ul. Lwowska 25-29: part of the ghetto wall with a commemorative plaque
5. The ghetto wall behind the school, Ul. Limanowskiego 62
6. Oskar Schindler's enamel dish factory, Ul. Lipowa 4
7. The ruins ot the pre-burial hall on Ul. Abrahama
8. The 'grey' house, Ul. Jerozolimska 3
9. Płaszów camp commander Amon Goeth's former villa, Ul. Heltmana 22
10. Memorial in honour of murdered Poles
11. Memorial to Jews murdered in the Płaszów camp

ROUTE 3:

PLAC BOHATERÓW GETTA (PLAC ZGODY) – PŁASZÓW

Plac Bohaterów Getta

Immediately after the bridge is Plac Bohaterów Getta, known before the Second World War as Plac Zgody, which was where the Jews were corralled before deportation to the concentration and death camps – mainly Bełżec and Auschwitz-Birkenau.

It is a place soaked in the blood of the Kraków Jews murdered by the Germans during the expulsions of June and October 1942 and at the time of the liquidation of the ghetto on 14 March 1943. On that day many Jewish men, women and children also met their deaths at the hands of the Nazis in the backyards and alleys around Plac Bohaterów Getta. In July 1948 the town council named the square Plac Bohaterów Getta to honour the memory of the victims. The square owes its current appearance to a redevelopment in 2005 financed by the President and City Council of Kraków and carried out to the design of the architects Piotr Lewicki and Kazimierz Łatak. In 1941-3 between the old bus station, standing alone at the northern extreme of Plac Bohaterów Getta, and the corner building on Ul. Kącik stood one of the ghetto gates. Close to the bus station there was a path for those on foot and on the road stood the entrance gates. This was the busiest pedestrian – and food smuggling – route with columns of workers going out to their places of work outside the ghetto. Tram number three from

The main gates of the Kraków ghetto from Rynek Podgórski, circa 1942

Kraków to Łagiewniki ran this way. It did not stop in the ghetto.

Before the Second World War more than 64,000 Jews lived in Kraków and this was a quarter of the city's population. Over 48,000 of them were driven out in the forced resettlements of the second half of 1940 and the early months of 1941. The Germans shut those who remained in a ghetto established in the right bank Kraków district of Podgórze. To March 20 1941 there were 15,000 Jews there and its population fluctuated, rising at times to 18,000. They were crammed into three-hundred-and-twenty, mostly one and two-storey, buildings. The ghetto was enclosed by a high wall with four gates with the main gate in Podgórze market square. On it was a huge Star of David and a Yiddish inscription, Jidisher wojnbecirk – Jewish housing estate. A tramline ran through it but no one got on or off there. After a time all the Jewish institutions were removed to the ghetto: the council, the hospital, the Jewish Mutual Aid Society, the orphanages, a post office, a pharmacy and an agency of the German Employment Office. In June and October 1942 there were mass deportations from the ghetto to the death camps, and with each its area was reduced. On 13 and 14 March 1943 the ghetto was liquidated with the old, the sick and the children either killed where they stood or taken to Auschwitz-Birkenau. Those able to

The liquidation of the Kraków ghetto 13 March 1943 Ul. Lwowska: the way to the Płaszów camp

work were taken to the forced labour camp at nearby Płaszów.

At Plac Bohaterów Getta 18 is the Museum of National Remembrance. It was established on 22 April 1983 in the former Pod Orłem (Under the Eagle) pharmacy. In 1941–43 it was inside the ghetto and was run to the end by its Polish owner, Tadeusz Pankiewicz. He was the only Pole the Germans allowed

The liquidation of the Kraków ghetto, ul Lwowska, 13 March 1943

The City of Kraków History Museum at the Pharmacy Under the Eagle

to stay permanently in the Jewish area. Pankiewicz witnessed everyday life in the ghetto and saw the Jews deported from Plac Zgody, where the journey to the death camps began. He wrote an extraordinary book documenting German crimes against the Kraków Jews called *Apteka w getcie krakowskim* (The Pharmacy in the Kraków Ghetto). The museum has permanent exhibitions devoted to the torment of the Jews in the ghetto and in the Płaszów concentration camp, and to Tadeusz Pankiewicz.

The building on the corner of Plac Bohaterów Getta and Ul. Piwna sheltered one of the contact points for the Jewish Combat Organization in the Kraków ghetto and this is commemorated by a plaque mounted on the wall in 1948. The Jewish Combat Organization in Kraków was established as a result of an agreement involving the Zionist youth organizations *Akiba* and *Dror-Frajhajt* and the Jewish group of the Polish Workers' Party. At the very top of the organisation were Adolf Liebeskind (Dolek) and Szymon Dränger (Marek Zborowski) from *Akiba*, Abraham Leibowicz (Laban, Romek) from *Dror-Frajhajt* as well as Hersz Bauminger (Bazyli), Gola Mirer (Lidka) and Beniamin Halbreich (Benek) from the Polish Workers' Party. Aware that they were involved in an unequal struggle, the young fighters employed a series of diversionary tactics and ambushes on the enemy. A number of attacks were carried out on 22 December 1942, of which the most effective was that on the Germans in the *Cyganeria* (Bohemia)

Apteka w getcie krakowskim

The exhibition at the Pharmacy Under the Eagle

Plaque on the corner of Plac Bohaterów Getta and Ul. Piwna commemorating a contact point for the Jewish Combat Organization in the Kraków ghetto

coffee house. This audacious move sent shockwaves through the city and beyond. Unfortunately, despite the great determination of its soldiers, the Jewish Combat Organization in Kraków was utterly smashed by the Gestapo. The majority of those involved in the *Cyganeria* raid were arrested while the others left the city. On the front of the building is a commemorative plaque which reads, 'To the memory of the heroes and martyrs of the Kraków ghetto murdered by the barbarian Germans. The base of operations of the Jewish Combat Organization was in this house. This plaque was mounted by the citizens committee on the fifth anniversary of the liquidation of the ghetto 13 March 1948.'

The main ghetto gate used to stand where Ul. Limanowskiego meets

Ul. Józefińska 18: while the ghetto existed the home of the Jewish Mutual Aid Organisation

Rynek Podgórski. The German police station and the Board of the Jewish Community were to be found in the corner building at Rynek Podgórski 1. In September 1939, shortly after occupying Kraków, the Germans dissolved the Jewish Community and established a Jewish Council (Judenrat) in its place, which was directly controlled by the Gestapo security police. In no respect was this a continuation of the pre-war institution, but merely the puppet body exclusively responsible for the swift and efficient execution of orders given by the German authorities. These included conducting censuses, supplying gangs of workers for forced labour, supervision of displaced persons and the organization of the expulsion of many tens of thousands of Jews from the city at the

Rynek Podgórski 1: while the ghetto existed the meeting place of the Board of the Jewish Community

end of 1941 and the beginning of 1942. After the establishment of the ghetto in March 1941 the Jewish Council's duties included maintaining order in the Jewish district, which they achieved with the aid of the Jewish Police (*Jüdisches Ordnungsdiens*) established for that purpose, ensuring food supplies and health and sanitary care, opposing resistance movements in the ghetto and assisting in the expulsions to the death camps.

The members of the Jewish Council had certain privileges: along with their families they generally were not subject to expulsions and they also had easier access to food rations. Despite this, its first two leaders, Dr Marek Biberstein and his successor, Dr Artur Rosenzweig, both paid with their lives for succumbing to the human emotions that prompted them to respond with insufficient zeal in carrying out the orders of their German masters. After the Ghetto's liquidation the members of the Jewish Council and their families were sent to work in the Optima and Madritsch workshops and, a few months later, were removed to the Płaszów forced labour camp.

Near to the Board of the Jewish Community were the two workshops mentioned above, which employed Jewish workers to sew army uniforms. One, at Rynek Podgórski 3, was owned

The building which once housed the Optima factory

Naczyń Emaliowanych i Wyrobów Blaszanych Rekord sp. z o.o.) moved from the nearby Ul. Romanowicza into a new factory shed at Ul. Lipowa 4. In November 1939 in the third month of the German occupation of Kraków the factory was renamed *Deutsche Emailwarenfabrik* and Oskar Schindler, Sudeten German, NSDAP member and industrialist, became its manager.

by Julius Madritsch, and the second, Optima, a chocolate factory before the war, lay between Ul. Węgierska 3 and Ul. Krakusa 7. Optima is remembered for the suffering of Jews who were rounded up there from 6 June 1942 and kept in a severe heat wave, with neither food nor water, until they were finally deported from the ghetto on 8 June.

We now return to the main route of our journey.

From Plac Bohaterów Getta we walk along Ul. Kącik and through the subway under the railway embankment to Ul. Lipowa. In 1938 the First Małopolska Enamel Dish and Tin Products Factory (*Pierwsza Małopolska Fabryka*

The factory enjoyed a period of prosperity under wartime conditions. The decisive factors in this were the free labour provided by the Jewish workers and the production of mess tins, cartridge cases for armour-piercing ordnance, and bomb fuses for the German army. From 1943 the factory's Jewish workers were accommodated in a camp built near to the factory that was administered as part of the forced labour camp at Płaszów. In 1944, while the Płaszów camp was being liquidated, Oskar Schindler secured the agreement of the German authorities to move his factory to Brünnlitz in the Sudetes. Around 1,100 Kraków

Office of the Oskar Schindler enamel dish factory at Ul. Lipowa 4, now a branch of the Kraków Museum of History

Jews found their way there. They included not only the factory's permanent workforce, but also others who were able to leave thanks to the document drawn up for that purpose: Schindler's list. All of them lived to see the end of the Second World War in Brünnlitz and their saviour was later honoured by Yad Vashem, The Holocaust Martyrs' and Heroes' Remembrance Authority, as Righteous Among the Nations. The wartime fate of Schindler's factory and its Jewish workers first entered popular consciousness via Thomas Keneally's book, Schindler's List, and later became known throughout the world thanks to Steven Spielberg's film of the same name shot in Kraków in 1993. In the

administrative building of the former factory there is now a branch of the Kraków Museum of History with an exhibition devoted to the story of Kraków and the fate of its Polish and Jewish inhabitants during the German occupation of 1939-45. The exhibition also portrays Kraków and its citizens in the years leading up to the outbreak of the Second World War.

We return once more to Plac Bohaterów Getta and proceed along Ul. Lwowska. This was once one of the main arteries of Podgórze but is now,

Ul. Lwowska 25-29 part of the ghetto wall with a commemorative plaque

following changes in the transport system, a side street. It leads in the direction of Płaszów and it was down this street that, in March 1943, columns of Kraków Jews were led under the escort of German soldiers to the Płaszów concentration camp. Between the buildings on Ul. Lwowska at numbers 25-29 lies a relic of the Kraków ghetto wall, a fragment of the system of ramparts, walls and barriers erected by the Germans to detach and isolate the Jewish district that existed in Podgórze in 1941-43. In 1983 a commemorative plaque was raised on the wall with inscriptions in Yiddish and Polish, 'Here they lived, suffered and died at the hands of the German torturers. Here they began their final journey to the death camps. This is a part of the Kraków ghetto wall, 1941-43'.

Ul. Lwowska runs into Ul. Limanowskiego and where this street ends was the border of the ghetto. Here, the wall turned westwards towards the Krzemionki Hills. Part of it has survived behind the Second Primary School at Ul. Limanowskiego 62. This section is tens of metres long and two metres high. Like the wall in Ul. Lwowska it is topped by semi-circular arches on all of its segments.

We now leave the area of the former ghetto and proceed along Ul.

The ghetto wall behind the school at Ul. Limanowskiego 62

Limanowskiego into Ul. Wielicka. We then turn right into Ul. Jerozolimska and reach the Płaszów concentration camp. (We can also take the tram, get off at Cmentarz Podgórski and cross the road to Ul. Jerozolimska).

A column of prisoners at the Płaszów concentration camp

The Płaszów concentration camp was first established at the end of 1942 as a penal forced labour camp. At its greatest extent it occupied around eighty hectares between Ul. Wielicka and Ul. Swoszowicka. It was enclosed by two electrified, barbed wire fences attached to upright poles with guard towers every few hundred metres. Both Poles and Jews were imprisoned there, but in different sectors. There were about 1,000 Polish prisoners – a figure which climbed heavily during the Warsaw Rising in the summer of 1944. The Jewish area, which was bigger, was divided into a number of sectors. There was a living area with separate buildings for men and women, an assembly point, an industrial area with workshops, a 'hospital' with several barracks for the sick, a quarantine barracks with individual places and a food area. Other than this there was a transport sector with vehicle workshops, stables and a coach house, an administrative sector with the commander's headquarters, pens for livestock and housing for the Germans. A railway station was built beyond the wire. The prisoners toiled in the workshops, in the quarry, and also outside the camp in a nearby cable factory in Płaszów and in a number of firms in the Zabłocie area. These included the German Oskar Schindler's enamel dish factory at Ul. Lipowa 4.

In mid-1943 the Płaszów camp became a branch of the Majdanek camp in Lublin and from January 1944 a concentration camp in its own right with branches at Wieliczka and Mielec. This meant that Jews from small camps and ghettos liquidated by the Germans, including Tarnów, Mielec, Rzeszów, Drohobycz, Janów and Szebnie near Jasło, were brought there, along with some Hungarian Jews. From Płaszów they were sent on to work in arms factories across the General-Gouvernement, including Skarżysko-Kamienna, Starachowice, Pionki and Częstochowa, and to the Reich and other concentration camps such as Auschwitz, Mauthasen and Gross-Rosen.

The Płaszów camp claimed many victims. The prisoners were enfeebled by hunger and illness, beaten, and exhausted by overwork. Of course, execution was a possibility at all times. There are several mass graves on the site of the camp with thousands of people buried in them. The Germans

General view of the Płaszów concentration camp

had planned to build a crematorium there to burn the dead bodies and even transported the equipment and materials needed. But they did not finally manage to set it up.

Among the Płaszów camp murderers Amon Goeth, the camp commandant, was particularly brutal in setting an example to his underlings of how to treat the prisoners. He shot many people himself and had done this before when the ghettos in Kraków, Tarnów and Szebnie were liquidated. After the war he was prosecuted by the Supreme National Tribunal in Kraków, and was found guilty of killing and persecution and sentenced to hang. The sentence was carried out on 13 September 1946. The witnesses' testimonies suggested that in the camp's early phase there were about 2,000 people there, rising to 10,000 and then to 25,000. The exact number of Jews killed in Płaszów, or removed from there and killed elsewhere, is difficult to establish. The lists of Jews taken from Płaszów to Auschwitz-Birkenau are now kept in the archives of the state museum in Auschwitz. But these generally concern those not killed in the gas chambers immediately on arrival but instead assigned numbers and made prisoners. Around 2,000 people survived evacuation from Płaszów. Among

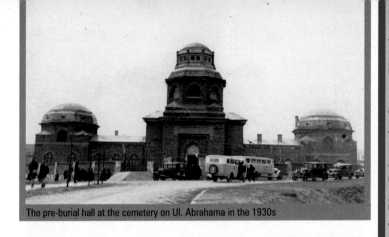

The pre-burial hall at the cemetery on Ul. Abrahama in the 1930s

these were around 1,000 people – seven hundred men and three hundred women – saved by Oskar Schindler, the owner of the enamel dish factory, who mainly employed Jews. In October 1944, thanks to him, they were taken from Kraków to spend the rest of the war in Brünnlitz (Brnenec) in the Sudetenland.

The Płaszów camp was established on the site of the Kraków and Podgórze Jewish cemeteries, whose addresses were Ul. Abrahama 3 (The Kraków Jewish Community's most recent cemetery established in 1932) and Ul. Jerozolimska 25 (The Podgórze Jewish Community Cemetery). While the camp was being established in 1942-3 these cemeteries were completely destroyed during levelling works, while the gravestones were used to make the roads firmer and as foundations for barracks. At the cemetery there was a monumental pre-burial house built by Adolf Siódmak. It was a triaxial building with characteristic cupolas covering its central section and both wings. The Jews hid antique liturgical objects from the Kraków synagogues in one of the copulas. These included cloths, metal objects and around one-hundred-and-fifty parchment scrolls of the Torah. They had been brought from the Jewish Community's headquarters at Ul. Limanowskiego 2 in the ghetto, where

121

The 'grey' house, Ul. Jerozolimska 3

they could at any minute have been con-fiscated. When the camp was finished the Germans used the pre-burial house as stables for horses and livestock, and as a pigsty. Later, when a railway branch line had been built to the camp the sta-bles were moved elsewhere and part of the pre-burial house was blown up. Unfortunately the objects the Jews had hidden in one of the cupolas were found by the Germans. Some were damaged by fire and others were taken to the East German Institute. (Stendig, *Dewastacja* p. 189, Bieberstein *Zagłada*, p. 228).

The area where the camp was is now derelict and neglected and there is not a single signpost that would make it easier to get around it and reach the sites of the mass graves or the relics of the Jewish cemetery and pre-burial house. One may begin, though, from the important point of orientation that is the house that stands alone at no.3 Ul. Jerozolimska, where it meets Ul. Heltmana and Ul. Abrahama. It was built in the 1920s to house workers from the cemetery and is known as the 'grey house', where SS men of notorious brutality lived while the camp was in existence, 'SS men Hujar, Zdrojewski, Landsdorfer, Ekert and Glaser [...] and in the cellar there was a prison – not an everyday one but an underground tor-ture chamber. Whoever was delivered

Płaszów camp commander Amon Goeth's former villa, Ul. Heltmana 22

The grave of Sara Schenirer

into the expert grip of this establishment never left it under their own steam' (Bau, *Czas zbezczeszczenia*, p. 127). Ul. Heltmana, which is an extension of Ul. Jerozolimska, was known in the camp's time as SS Strasse because German officers had houses there, including the villa of camp commandant Amon Leopold Goeth.

We leave Ul. Jerozolimska along the unsurfaced road next to the 'grey house' and then turn right onto a grass path running behind it. We quickly reach the isolated gravestone of Sara Schenirer (1883-1935) who, in 1917, founded in Kraków the *Bejt Jakow* school for girls from Orthodox families.

The destruction of the pre-burial hall on Ul. Abrahama in Podgórze, 1944

Her original memorial was destroyed during the building of the camp and the present one was placed here in 2005. Continuing along the path through the grass we reach the ruin of the pre-burial house. Its construction began in 1926 yet it was not completely finished when the Second World War broke out. It was a monumental, triaxial building with striking oriental accents and featured three sizeable cupolas, with the central one resting on a high, eight-sided tambour. In 1943 the building was desacralized by its use as a horse stable, as a cowshed and as a pigpen (Bieberstein, *Zagłada* p. 228). In 1944 the Germans blew up the pre-burial house in connection with extending the camp and building a railway branch line to it.

The commandant at that time, Amon Leopold Goeth, turned this into a dramatic spectacle and event by inviting numerous observers along to witness it. Following this, only the left wing was salvaged, which housed a hydrophore station supplying the camp with water. This part of the pre-burial hall survived until 1947 before finally sharing the fate of the rest of the building.

Taking the same path for another 100-120 metres we reach the remains of the Jewish cemetery in Podgórze which consist of fifteen or twenty grave footings but only one gravestone. This bears an inscription in Hebrew and Polish telling of the burial here of Chaim Jakub Abrahamer, son of Izaak Meir, who died in 1932. Next, we return in

Remembrance march

the direction of the 'grey house' and turn right onto what remains of the un-surfaced Ul. Abrahama. In the years of the camp's existence it was known as Bergenstrasse and ran through the cen-tre of the camp. A short way along is a memorial that was raised in 1984 to the memory of thirteen Poles murdered by the Nazis in the first mass execution in Kraków of the Second World War on 10 September 1939.

On the left there are the limestone hills which were the site of the Płaszów camp's quarry. The stones were broken by prisoners chosen for the penal com-pany, while the slave labour involved

Memorial in honour of Jews murdered in the Płaszów concentration camp

in moving them was done by twenty or thirty Jewish and Polish women harnessed to three railway wagons.

We now reach the ridge of the hill and follow it parallel to Ul. Abrahama towards a large monument which is visible further on. To the left we can see a high cross erected on the site of one of the Płaszów camp's mass graves. We then reach the monument we first mentioned after passing two smaller ones. To the right is one erected by Kraków Jews and on the plaque of the stone obelisk is the inscription, 'Here, on this spot, in the years 1943-45, thousands of Jews brought here from Poland and Hungary were tortured, murdered and incinerated'.

We do not know their names, but let us replace them with one: the Jews. Here, in this place, one of the most severe crimes was committed. Human language knows no words to describe its atrocity, its unspeakable bestiality, its ruthlessness or its cruelty. Let us replace them with one word: Nazism. The Jews who survived the Nazi pogrom pay homage to the memory of those murdered, whose final scream of despair is this Płaszów cemetery's silence'.

To the left is a statue that was unveiled in 2000 and pays tribute to the Hungarian Jewish women who were processed by the Płaszów concentration camp on their way to the gas chambers at Auschwitz-Birkenau.

The largest of the monuments is one raised to all the nationalities murdered by the Germans in the Płaszów camp. It was designed by Witold Cęckiewicz and was unveiled on 4 September 1964. Its inscription reads, 'In memory of the martyrs murdered in the Nazi genocide of 1939-45'.

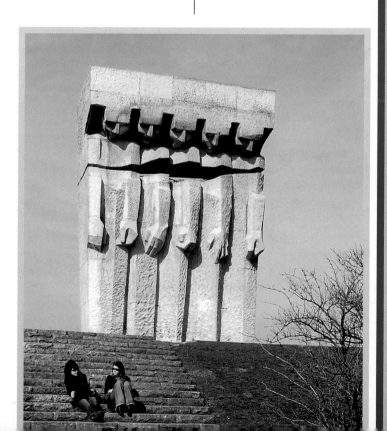

A Selected Bibliography

Bałaban, *Przewodnik* – Majer Bałaban, *Przewodnik po żydowskich zabytkach Krakowa,* [A Guide to the Jewish Monuments and Historical Buildings of Kraków] Nakładem Stowarzyszenia „Solidarność – B'nei B'rith" w Krakowie, Kraków – 1935.

Bałaban, *Historia* – Majer Bałaban, *Historia Żydów w Krakowie i na Kazimierzu,* [A History of the Jews in Kraków and Kazimierz, II Vols.] *T. I :1304-1655,* Kraków 1931, *T. II: 1656-1868,* Kraków 1936, Wyd. „Nadzieja".

Bau, *Czas zbezczeszczenia* – Józef Bau, *Czas zbezczeszczenia. Wspomnienia z czasów drugiej wojny światowej,* [A Time of Profanation: Memories from the Second World War] Wydawnictwo 'Hamena'anea', Tel-Aviv 1990.

Bieberstein, *Zagłada* – Aleksander Bieberstein, *Zagłada Żydów w Krakowie,* [The Extermination of the Jews in Kraków] Wydawnictwo Literackie, Kraków 1985.

Döblin, *Podróż po Polsce* – Alfred Döblin, *Podróż po Polsce.* [Journey through Poland] Wydawnictwo Literackie, Kraków 2000.

Gross, *Żydowski bard* – Natan Gross, *Żydowski bard. Gawęda o życiu i twórczości Mordechaja Gebirtiga,* [The Jewish Bard: a Miscellany of the Life and Work of Mordechaj Gebirtig] Księgarnia Akademicka, Kraków 2000.

Pankiewicz, *Apteka* – Tadeusz Pankiewicz, *Apteka w getcie krakowskim,* [The Pharmacy in the Kraków Ghetto] Instytut Wydawniczy „Świat i Wiedza", Kraków 1947.

Stendig, *Dewastacja* – Jakub Stendig, *Dewastacja cmentarzy, bóżnic i zabytków żydowskich Krakowa podczas okupacji hitlerowskiej* [The Devastation of Cemeteries, Temples and Monuments of Jewish Kraków during the Nazi Occupation. (In) On the Third Anniversary of the Liquidation of the Jewish Ghetto 13/3/1943 – 13/3/1946] [w:] *W 3-cią rocznicę zagłady ghetta w Krakowie (13. III. 1943 – 13. III. 1946),* Kraków 1946.

Żydzi w Krakowie – *Żydzi w Krakowie. Życie i zagłada starodawnej gminy,* (pod red. S. Lesera), [Jews in Kraków: the Life and Extermination of a Departed Community, S. Leser ed.] Wyd. Stowarzyszenie Krakowian w Hajfie, wydanie 2, Hajfa 1983.